Coming Out of the Republican Closet

Coming to Terms with
Being Black, Patriotic, and Conservative

REGINALD BOHANNON

Thanks for your support!

[signature]

TRAFFORD
PUBLISHING
USA · Canada · UK · Ireland

Corrections

Pg 17, line 25: change "did" to "did not"

Pg 34, line 28, change "crosses" to "headstones"

Pg 35, lines 2, 10 & 24 change "crosses" to "headstones"

Front and back cover photos by Bovanti Photography – bovanti.com. Make-up by Taylor Bohannon featuring Bovanti Cosmetics. Set Design by Reginald Bohannon, Jr.

Book editing by Integrity Editorial Services

Note for Librarians: A cataloguing record for this book is available from Library and Archives Canada at www.collectionscanada.ca/amicus/index-e.html
ISBN 1-4120-7939-X

Printed in Victoria, BC, Canada. Printed on paper with minimum 30% recycled fibre. Trafford's print shop runs on "green energy" from solar, wind and other environmentally-friendly power sources.

PUBLISHING™
Offices in Canada, USA, Ireland and UK
This book was published *on-demand* in cooperation with Trafford Publishing. On-demand publishing is a unique process and service of making a book available for retail sale to the public taking advantage of on-demand manufacturing and Internet marketing. On-demand publishing includes promotions, retail sales, manufacturing, order fulfilment, accounting and collecting royalties on behalf of the author.

Book sales for North America and international:
Trafford Publishing, 6E–2333 Government St.,
Victoria, BC v8t 4p4 CANADA
phone 250 383 6864 (toll-free 1 888 232 4444)
fax 250 383 6804; email to orders@trafford.com
Book sales in Europe:
Trafford Publishing (uk) Limited, 9 Park End Street, 2nd Floor
Oxford, UK ox1 1hh UNITED KINGDOM
phone 44 (0)1865 722 113 (local rate 0845 230 9601)
facsimile 44 (0)1865 722 868; info.uk@trafford.com
Order online at:
trafford.com/05-2837

10 9 8 7 6 5 4 3

Dedicated to my wonderful family: Mom, Deborah, Lillian, Michael, Reginald, Jr. and Taylor.

To Peggy, the love of my life.

Acknowledgements

First and foremost, I would like to acknowledge my loving parents, Edward J. Bohannon and Margaret A. Bohannon, and my caring grandparents, Reverend R.Q. Allen and Zala Allen. Mom, you have been quite instrumental in heightening my interest in politics. Your grassroots efforts in politics over the years have truly been an education in political science.

To my brother Michael and your lovely wife, Anita, as well as your two beautiful daughters, Marquis and Marquel, thanks for putting up with my minority viewpoints on political issues and for listening and being a sounding board for me.

My two sisters, Deborah and Lillian, have been wonderful to me. Deborah, regardless of my political leanings, you are still willing to listen to me. Lillian, we are already on the same page politically, and for that I say thanks.

Reginald Jr. and Taylor, you are two loving children. You two are truly becoming great patriots, particularly with your volunteer work at the National Museum of Patriotism. Taylor, your singing rendition of the Constitution's preamble is a number one hit.

Peggy, you certainly have been a trouper in being subjected to my political rantings. You have been supportive as well as instrumental in getting my book off the ground. You have been with me from the beginning of this project. Thanks, Peggy. I love you.

Raynard and Ken, I miss you.

Table of Contents

Preface

Toastmasters **Ice-Breaker Speech: Patriotism**
(June 12, 2002)

Good afternoon, everyone! I decided to write my speech on something that is near and dear to me and is a great part of my character—patriotism. I was a Boy Scout and I am an Air Force veteran of seven years; four of those years I spent working with the Air Force One Presidential Wing in Washington, D.C. The Boy Scouts, where I started as a tyro in the subject of patriotism, taught me a great deal about what a patriot is, and the Air Force allowed me to carry out my patriotism.

In honor of our holiday on Friday, Flag Day, as well as Independence Day next month, I felt this would be an opportune time for me to share some of my thoughts and feelings on the United States flag and the greatest legal document ever written—the United States Constitution.

As I hold up this flag and lighter, what would your reaction be if I set the flag on fire? Do I even have the right legally to set it on fire? Some people would say that I do have the right to set it ablaze, while others would say I do not.

The truth is, I do have the right to burn Old Glory; that's one of the freedoms that we enjoy here in the United States. But you can't legally start fires just anywhere. I think the Equity Office personnel would be displeased if I started a fire here in their building. Now, if I was somewhere where fires can be started, like at home or at a cookout, then I legally have the right to burn the flag. But even knowing that it is legal to do so in certain places, if I was in the presence of someone trying to burn a serviceable flag, they would have a skirmish with me on their hands. Flag burning in my presence is something that I will not tolerate.

And this is just one of the dichotomies of our country. We have so many liberties here in the United States. We have the right not to be patriotic. We have the freedom to choose our religion, as well as to choose our leaders through elections. We even have the freedom to chastise our elected statesmen and our government. There are very few countries around the world where people can do that.

Thomas Jefferson penned the Declaration of Independence, and the most memorable part states, "We hold these truths to be self–evident, that all men are created equal, that they are endowed by their Creator with certain unalienable Rights, that among these are Life, Liberty and the pursuit of Happiness."

And quoting Alexander Hamilton, "The Declaration of Independence was the promise; the Constitution was the fulfillment."

When the Constitution was ratified, segments of it initially did not apply to everyone, especially minorities and women. But as time went on, forward thinkers such as abolitionist William Lloyd Garrison and future Supreme Court Justice Thurgood Marshall held America's feet to the fire and eventually proved that it did pertain to every American. Now, through amendments, we all enjoy the same rights the Constitution affords.

But let me ask, just what is patriotism? One definition of a patriot is one who loves his or her country, and defends and promotes its interests. I consider myself to fit into this category. In saying that, I do not mean that I love or would defend every action of our government. Slavery is something that I would not endorse. Women not being able to vote is something else I would not support. Going back to the Founding Fathers, one insightful vision they had was Article 5 of the Constitution, which allows for amendments to it. Fortunately, the 13th Amendment abolished slavery and the 19th Amendment approved of women's suffrage.

So whether or not you are a patriot, historical documents such as the Constitution and the Declaration of Independence can be instrumental in you deciding the side of constitutional issues on which you will fall. When you exercise your right of suffrage, the right to vote, these documents can be helpful to you if you know how the candidates view and adhere to them.

Speaking of the Declaration of Independence, a copy of one of the two hundred or so originals that was printed in 1776 is currently on display at the Jimmy Carter Presidential Library.

Since the tragic attacks of September 11, a great majority of Americans has gotten back to their day-to-day activities—which, in a sense, is a good thing. But it would be nice if, throughout our day-to-day activities, we would take time out to think of and say a prayer for the ones whose lives are not back to normal—people such as our own friend and colleague, Mosi, who is fighting a war, shores away from us, ensuring that we can go back to enjoying our freedom, like being risk specialists, entertainers, workaholics, or just plain couch potatoes. An e-mail, a care package, or a letter or two from home would be greatly appreciated by our defenders of freedom.

Appreciate Flag Day this Friday and enjoy Independence Day next month.

May God bless America.

Introduction

On the train to and from my 9-to-5 job in Atlanta, I sometimes contemplate my life in the political arena—not as a politician, but as a citizen of this great country. I ponder how my views on politics have evolved over the years. I went from not caring about politics at all, to taking a modicum of interest in my family-chosen party (Democratic), to asking myself whether I really was a liberal or a closet conservative who was just too embarrassed to admit it.

If I was embarrassed, it was because there is such widespread antipathy to the Republican Party in the black community. There is a saying that goes something like this: "When you are young and broke, you join the Democratic Party; when you get older and start making money, you switch to the Republican Party." There is another saying in the black community: "My parents and grandparents were Democrats, so I am a Democrat." Then there's another saying: "If you are black and Republican, you are a *sellout*." Sometimes the word sellout in that saying is replaced with the term *Uncle Tom*; Harry Belafonte even used the term *house slave*.

Despite this antipathy, I wrote this book because I felt compelled to get my story out to the public. I have come across quite a few people, particularly blacks, who have stories similar to mine but who, just like me, did not want to speak out because of the potential backlash. It was clear that if one of us were to write a book about our experiences, he or she surely would receive a lot of criticism. That being the case, I decided courageously to let it be me.

I also wrote this book because I feel it was destiny, more

like God's will, for me to do so. By destiny, I mean that I was being prepared for this task without realizing it.

For instance, I joined Toastmasters on a whim, not thinking about how the skills I would obtain through that organization would aid me greatly in speaking out publicly about my conservative transformation. Toastmasters gave me the confidence to speak about my beliefs, for which I am passionate.

Later, I enrolled in Herzing College to finish the degree I started years earlier while in the Air Force. The courses I have taken at Herzing include English, speech, and psychology, all very helpful when writing a book.

During the past twelve to thirteen years, I have struggled with my politics. Through the books I have read, the historical documents I have dusted off and pored over, and the knowledge I have gained during these years, I have come to grips with the fact that I am a conservative—a Republican. Now I am putting pen to paper and also saying out loud to anyone who cares to listen that I am out of the closet! Follow along with me, but please, hold off on the name calling until you hear me out.

1

Growing Up in the Graveyard

———◆———

My family is from Lexington, North Carolina, a small town in the Piedmont Triad, about a forty-five-minute drive up Interstate 85 from "the Queen City," Charlotte. "'The Ton,'" as Lexington is affectionately called, is famous for its furniture-making and some of the world's best pork barbecue; just ask the food critics at the *Wall Street Journal* or numerous restaurant magazines and food television shows. Just as Chicago, Atlanta, and other cities have painted cows, Lexington has painted pigs all around town.

Lexington was settled in 1775 and named after Lexington, Massachusetts, which is famous for its battle in the Revolutionary War. The city was incorporated in 1828 and celebrated its 175th anniversary in 2003. Lexington is the county seat of Davidson County, named for General William Lee Davidson of Revolutionary War fame.

One of the more famous individuals from Lexington is Bob

Timberlake, the internationally renowned artist and home-furnishings designer. I can recall my neighborhood friend Buddy, who was a classmate of Bob's son, taking me over to the Timberlakes' house. Seeing all the landscape paintings around the house was something special.

Another Lexingtonian who gained fame is Charles Moose, who was chief of police in Montgomery County, Maryland, during the sniper-shooting incidents in the Washington, D.C., area in 2002. Initially, many Lexingtonians were proud of the fact that a fellow Lexingtonian was on the case, especially when the snipers were caught. Once his book came out, though, some people's opinions of him changed. It seemed that his memory of Lexington was somewhat different from that of some others who grew up there. I and some of my family members—including my mother, who is of Moose's parents' generation—did not agree with his recollection of the Ku Klux Klan's presence in our neighborhood. Chief Moose wrote about a boundary that we could not cross for fear of the KKK. If there was a boundary, we trampled all over it.

April 4, 1968, was a sad and awful day for the country, including Lexington. That day, we got the tragic news that Dr. Martin Luther King, Jr. had been shot. I was 7 years old at the time, and Dr. King's assassination is the first historical event for which I can remember where I was when it happened. Our yellow wall phone rang and Mom picked it up. All of a sudden, Mom said, "Dr. King has been shot!" Mom truly was hurt. At some point in time, a riot broke out in uptown Lexington, just as riots broke out in other cities across the country. One of our family friends came to our house and told us about it. He said something like, "Don't go uptown because they are rioting and the National Guard is up there!" Things eventually calmed down.

Edward Julustus Bohannon, my father, and Margaret Ann Bohannon, my mother, had five kids. Deborah and Lillian are my older sisters. Michael is my older brother. Raynard and I, my fraternal twin, were born August 5, 1960. Raynard passed away in February 1983.

Mom did most of the child-raising—she and Dad divorced when I was about 5 years old. After they divorced, Dad moved to New Jersey and then eventually to Virginia. He came home to visit us a couple of times a year. When the boys of the family got a little older, we went to visit Dad occasionally during the summer.

In a lot of divorced families, the kids miss the parent who is not there and, at the same time, harbor ill feelings toward the parent who is there doing the raising. This was true in my case, mainly because it was Mom who administered the discipline. Fortunately for me, these ill feelings dissipated the day I departed home to join the Air Force.

We grew up in a neighborhood called the Graveyard. Mom continues to live there today. The neighborhood consists of three streets: Biesecker Drive, Ulysses Street, and Grant Street. It seems that someone must have admired our eighteenth president. Grant Street, where we mainly grew up, has six modest brick homes. Over time, our family has lived on all three streets.

Our neighborhood was called the Graveyard because it was home to a city cemetery. That graveyard was also the source of our neighborhood ball team's nickname, "the Graveyard Boys." The graveyard had a road that divided it evenly into two football field-size tracts of land. One side was for graves, where my paternal grandparents are buried. The other side was for baseball, softball, and, of course, football for the neighborhood kids. At least, that was what we made it out to be. Virtually flat, it was the best unofficial football field in Lexington.

To this day, I can remember the sight of a backhoe digging a grave on "our" football field for the first time. This encroachment was not a pleasant sight for the Graveyard Boys, but at least it was at the opposite end of the field from where we played. Today, our football field holds the graves of former teammates and opponents, as well. Two of those former teammates include my beloved twin brother, Raynard, and my childhood "best friend," Ken. Knowing that we all die at some point in time, how heavenly it is to be buried in your own football field.

Raynard and I were great brothers to each other. When we were young, he was always much bigger than me. Whenever Mom took us uptown to shop for clothes, she bought him husky-size pants while I got the small size. In fact, people who did not know us well, but who knew there were twins in our family, assumed that Michael, who is three years older, was Raynard's twin.

In August 1966, Mom took Raynard and me to our school, South Lexington Elementary, to enter the first grade. Having our mom leave us on our first day of school was a little traumatic for both of us. Our saving grace was that we were together, but that didn't last long. When our teacher, Mrs. McCall, realized that we were twins, she stated that we had to be separated. I can remember her saying something like, "Oh no! We're going to have to separate you two. We can't have you two in the same class."

I never understood the separate-twins policy, but it kept us from having another class together until we shared an English class in our senior year at Lexington Senior High School. One consequence of this policy was that we established largely separate friendships throughout our school years. But even though we ran in separate circles, we had each other's back—he mainly mine—when it came to school fights. Raynard and I could fight each other before we left home in the morning for the school bus, but if we got to the bus stop and someone tried to jump on me, he was right there to help me fight my battles.

Knowing that he had my back gave me confidence and a little leeway in "talking trash" to my school enemies.

Fortunately, the Graveyard was not a ghetto. In fact, Lexington did not have much in the way of ghettos compared to bigger cities. That is not to say it was not tough for me growing up in the Graveyard. But my biggest mishaps were self-inflicted.

Once, while I was riding a bicycle down the hill on Biesecker Drive, I had an accident and was knocked unconscious. One of my neighbors, Ms. Jessie, revived me while I was stretched out in the middle of the street. Upon seeing the ambulance waiting for me, I slapped Ms. Jessie, jumped up, and ran home. In my adolescent mind, an ambulance was akin to death and I was not about to take a ride to my death. I later apologized to Ms. Jessie for slapping her.

Another childhood incident was even more bizarre. Ms. Jessie and Ms. Naomi, who lived together at the beginning of our street, owned several dogs, as well as a couple of chickens and roosters. One of Ms. Naomi's roosters was downright mean—just as nasty and vicious as any fowl you ever wanted to see. We called it "Super Chicken."

On numerous occasions when we neighborhood kids were walking home to the other end of our dirt street, Super Chicken chased us home. Then, one afternoon while I was walking home alone, I found a butter knife. I immediately got the bright idea of getting back at Super Chicken by throwing the butter knife at it in order to stab it.

I would meet Super Chicken on its own turf. I cut through my next door neighbor's back yard to get to Super Chicken's yard. I walked up to it and we faced each other off as if we were about to have a duel. I threw the knife at it, only to miss. Well, why did I do that? Super Chicken charged me quickly, flying up in my face and squawking. It happened so fast that I did not have time to turn around and retreat. The only thing I could do was backpedal, but I tripped over something and fell, hitting the back of my head on a cinder block. I got up and felt the back of my head cut and bloodied.

I walked home disgusted and defeated. Inside the house, I sneaked past Mom and some family guests and went straight into the bathroom to tend to my wounds. While in the bathroom, a gentleman walked in and immediately saw the blood. In a worried tone he said, "Boy, has your mom seen your head?" "No," I replied nervously. He called Mom into the bathroom to take a look at my head. Mom immediately got alarmed and somewhat hysterical. She said, "Reggie, what happened to you?" I said sheepishly, "I fell and hit my head on a brick." I did not even mention Super Chicken. We rushed into our station wagon and she quickly drove me to Lexington Memorial Hospital.

Mom had gone with me through bumps, bruises, and scrapes, but this was the first time I had seen her really worried about me, and it somewhat frightened me. I had to receive stitches for the first time, but looking at Mom, I thought the doctor was sewing my brain back inside my head.

Needless to say, I recovered. But I cannot say that about Super Chicken; I think it became someone's dinner soon after our duel.

*

Growing up in Lexington was very rewarding. Of course, when you are a kid, you long for big-city life, especially if you like sports. However, Major League Baseball, the NFL, and the NBA did not make Lexington home. For baseball, the Baltimore Orioles with Boog Powell came on television often on the weekends, which is why I am an Orioles fan to this day. The Redskins and the Dolphins were pretty much our football home teams. The Dolphins, with Bob Griese, Mercury Morris,

Larry Csonka, and company, became my team. The Carolina Cougars were our American Basketball Association team. But all you sports fans know about Atlantic Coast Conference basketball, and Lexington is in ACC country. David Thompson of North Carolina State University was my basketball hero in the early '70s.

Lexington was not Mayberry, but it was, and still is, a friendly town. Walking uptown on Main Street brought waves and greetings from people, both blacks and whites, whom you did not know. Lexingtonians were not necessarily strangers to one another, just fellow citizens whose names you did not know.

Remnants of segregation still had a grip on Lexington when I was a kid growing up in the '60s and '70s. The racial division was nowhere more prevalent than in our barbecue restaurants. I can recall going to eat at one barbecue restaurant where we would, out of habit, go to the back of the restaurant and place our orders to go. Eventually, both blacks and whites used the back door to place orders. If you wanted to eat in the restaurant, they gladly accommodated both blacks and whites. I don't know if this shows how ridiculous segregation was or if the restaurant owners eventually realized just how bad for business segregation was, but the restaurant was divided into two separate sides. One side was for black customers and the other side for white customers, with both sides being served the same great barbecue. Judge Henry Brown of the Plessey vs. Ferguson case would have been pleased with this separate-but-equal nonsense.

*

As far back as I can remember, Mom has voted and worked for the Democratic Party. She has been an allegiant Democrat since the early 1960s. She distributed campaign literature and paraphernalia such as buttons, fliers, and bumper stickers. Her collection of souvenirs includes candidate John F. Kennedy buttons, candidate Jimmy Carter bumper stickers, and candidate Bill Clinton fliers.

One of her many duties on the first Tuesday after the first Monday of November during election years was transporting voters to the polling sites. I can recall her picking up voters, blacks and whites, in our family station wagon and transporting them to polling precincts, including our school, South Lexington Elementary.

Most of the voters she transported were senior citizens who did not have transportation of their own. However, some of the voters she transported, perhaps unsavory characters, may not have been aware that it was Election Day. But they always knew who to vote for. On several occasions before elections, a black-slate flier, listing the politicians blacks were supposed to vote for, was disseminated in the black community.

Mom sometimes worked at the polling precincts, performing numerous tedious duties. On some occasions, she worked as a judge, ensuring that the ballots and paperwork were in order. Other times, she assisted the older voters in the booth, helping them turn the pages. Mom said some of the voters wanted her to mark or punch their ballots, but she said she was not allowed to do that.

Mom's most glorious and rewarding Democratic years were when William Jefferson Blythe Clinton was elected president. Mom was President Clinton's biggest fan (and still is). She absolutely adored him! I imagined that she loved him more than Mrs. Clinton.

Knowing how much Mom admired President Clinton, I wrote to the White House to request that a photo of President Clinton be sent to her. The staff complied by sending a photo of the president, plus photos of Buddy the dog and Socks the cat! All three photos hang in Mom's living room to this day.

Over the years, Mom has remained a loyal Democrat, through good and bad times for the party. But now that the Democrats are out of the White House and are the minority party in the House and Senate, politics are not very enjoyable for her. When President Clinton was in office, her favorite television stations were CNN, MSNBC, and C-SPAN. Now that President Bush is in the White House, the Food Channel has become her choice of viewing. Emeril Lagasse is one of the chefs she watches. These days, "Bam!" is heard much more than the gavel from C-SPAN's coverage of Congress.

My plan for the ultimate pick-me-up for Mom is for us to visit the William Clinton Presidential Library and Museum in Little Rock, Arkansas. It will not be one of my favorite activities, but in keeping with my respect for the presidential office and for my Mom, I can certainly do it.

During the Clinton administration, I would get word from my brother Mike or my sister Deborah that Mom was feeling a little down, so I would call her and debate politics. That would get her blood flowing! Discussing President Clinton, Hillary, Al Gore, and other Democrats would lift her spirits. Now I have to try a little harder to get her spirits up. I can't think of any good that would have come from Gore being elected president except that Mom's spirits would have been lifted.

Our debates don't cause us to want to come to blows, but they certainly get rambunctious from time to time. And when President Clinton was in office, I could never win! Sometimes Mom would hit below the belt, especially when she would say, "Reggie I don't see how you can be my son. I didn't raise you like that. I'm embarrassed you are my son!"

Over the years, Mom has been a true grass-roots soldier for the Democratic Party. For her tireless efforts, I contacted her congressman, Mel Watt of North Carolina, and placed an order for a United States flag to be flown over Capitol Hill on her 73rd birthday and sent to her as a gift from her family. Getting her this flag was an honor and privilege for me. Mom is a true citizen and was well deserving of a U.S. Capitol flag.

Even though Mom and I are on opposite sides politically, we love each other dearly. I will always love her and admire her commitment to her cause. After each of our debates, no matter how heated they get, we always end by saying "I love you, Mom" and "I love you too, Reggie."

*

Dad was a special person. Practically everyone in town called him Big Dad. By the early '90s, Dad had remarried. He and his wife, Paula, had moved back to Lexington. Their two-story blue house was a gathering place for young and old alike. If I had been younger at the time, I probably would have been jealous of everyone calling him Big Dad. But he was an easy-going person and well liked. Every time I would call him, he would say enthusiastically, "Hey Reggie!" He was always excited to hear from me, even if we had talked just the day before.

Dad was also a giving person. He loved fishing, especially deep-sea fishing. I recall him telling us about offering some fish he had caught to a man who was not doing well financially. The man asked, "Are you going to clean them?" Needless to say, Dad didn't clean the fish and the man didn't get any fish, either.

After Dad had been retired for some time, he and Paula decided to purchase a recreational vehicle to see the country. And see the country they did. My two children, Reggie and Taylor, received postcards from Dad and Paula from all across the country.

In 1995, they came to Atlanta in their deluxe RV for Thanksgiving to visit Michael and me and our families. All of us, especially the kids, loved their house on wheels. After the holidays, they headed to Florida in their RV for the winter, and I began thinking about joining them in Florida in March for the Atlanta Braves' spring training. However, about a month after they left, Paula called us with the sad news that Dad had passed away in his sleep.

Sad as it was that Dad had died, he taught me a great deal about living while he was alive. He taught me to live my own life, have fun, and enjoy your time here. This is truly a lesson that will never escape me. Love you, Dad.

*

My maternal grandparents were and still are a huge influence on my siblings and me, as well as countless other people. Both were pillars of our family and their community, besides being wonderful and cheerful grandparents. Granddad was first and foremost a pastor—Reverend Ralph Quincy Allen. He ministered at Goodwill Baptist Church in Arcadia, North Carolina. My grandmother, Zala Allen, or Ma Zala as she was known, was a homemaker and a businesswoman.

Granddad, born December 18, 1905, was a hard-working man. He and Ma Zala owned a few businesses, one of which was a "washateria" (a self-serve laundry) in Lexington. Their biggest business interest was rest homes. They owned and operated two rest homes for thirty-nine years. Both were in North Carolina, one in Gastonia and the other in Yadkin, out in the country off Route 64 near Lexington. The uniqueness of the rest home in Yadkin was that their home was attached to it. A hallway separated their house from the rest home.

In addition to being a pastor and a businessman, Granddad was a farmer. He and Ma Zala owned a very large farm, which we called the Ponderosa. The Yadkin rest home was on their farmland, and the crops they grew and the animals they raised supplied both rest homes with food year-round.

Granddad worked hard all the time. Farming, running rest homes, and ministering are all full-time jobs, and Granddad did them all well. Still, Granddad somehow found time for a hobby—hunting. He owned several guns, mostly shotguns and rifles. He, along with his brother, Uncle Coy, and others, hunted mainly rabbits, as I recall.

I never got to talk politics with Granddad and Ma Zala. The Lord called Ma Zala home on June 16, 1975, and Granddad joined her on June 4, 1992. I don't know if they were Republicans or Democrats. But I do know that they were hard-working entrepreneurs. And as a hunter and gun owner, Granddad certainly must have believed in the Constitution's Second Amendment. They were a God-fearing couple—after all, Granddad was a pastor for forty-two years. They were also loving grandparents and great Americans. May God bless their souls.

*

When I think about why I am such a patriot and have been for some time, I have to say that becoming a Boy Scout was the beginning. When my older brother Mike joined the Boy Scouts, naturally I wanted to follow in his footsteps. My problem was that I was not old enough. You have to be at least 11 years old, but I was only 10 at the time in 1970. Nevertheless, Scoutmaster Bill Williams allowed me to sit in on the weekly Monday evening meetings.

I had already begun studying and learning about Scouting by working with Mike and using his Boy Scout Handbook. The Scout Oath or Promise, the Scout Law, the Scout motto, and the Scout slogan are the rules of Scouting. This spirit of Scouting taught me about honor and my country.

Scoutmaster Bill was impressed that I had learned a good bit of this before actually becoming a member. He held me up as an example to other boys who were already members but had not yet learned the basics of Scouting.

Scouting put an emphasis on learning about our country and democracy. It taught me about my rights as a citizen, as well as my duties. We learned about our flag and its history. I enjoyed saluting the flag and learning how to fold it, as well as learning about the history of Lexington. The outdoors and camping aspect of Scouting was especially appealing to me. Building clubhouses in the woods near our home and staying with our grandparents on their farm had already introduced me to the wilderness and the great outdoors. When we were in the Boy Scouts, my grandparents allowed us to camp on their land. Once when we were camping on their land, it started raining quite heavily and continued virtually all night. Ma Zala worried about us getting sick, so she let us bring our sleeping bags inside. We slept in the rest home.

The Boy Scouts are not an overtly religious organization, as some would have people believe. Most of us Scouts went to church on our own. What the Boy Scouts did was reaffirm the presence of God in our lives. The Boy Scout Handbook states, "Your parents and religious leaders teach you about God, and the ways in which you can serve." So Scouting taught us tacitly that going to church was the right thing to do.

The Scout Law is a code of conduct that consists of twelve points to live by to make you a better person and man when you eventually become one. One of those points, "Reverent," means a Scout is "reverent toward God. He is faithful in his religious duties. He respects the beliefs of others." Following the Scout motto, "Be Prepared," and the Scout slogan, "Do a good turn daily," would benefit us all.

One day in the fall of 1974, our Boy Scout troop got the news that Scoutmaster Bill had died. It hit us very hard because he had been a father figure to all of us. Scouting just was not the same after he passed. Our troop somewhat lost its focus and drive. Along with some other Scouts, I soon drifted from Scouting. But even though I left Scouting, I consider it one of the pillars of my life.

*

In the fall of 1972, while I was in the seventh grade at Dunbar Intermediate School, my social studies class held a mock election for president of the United States. I did not follow politics at the time. George McGovern won the mock election. President Nixon received a measly two votes. One of my classmates admitted to voting for Nixon. My classmates were puzzled as to which classmate cast the other vote for Nixon. Well, former classmates, I am here admitting to you that it was I.

My first foray into politics came in the spring of 1973, when I was still in the seventh grade at Dunbar. Elections for our upcoming eighth-grade school year at Lexington Middle School were nearing. The middle school consisted of the eighth and ninth grades. The president would be a ninth-grader and the vice president an eighth-grader. One day in class, my teacher, Mr. Everhart, was discussing the upcoming election. He turned to me and said, "Reggie, why don't you run for vice president?"

I had not thought about running, especially since the ever-poplar Richard Strader had already thrown his hat into the ring. Richard's dad, Dr. Strader, was our family doctor; in fact, he had delivered Raynard and me. Unlike Richard, I was not all that popular at Dunbar, so we had to come up with a great strategy for the pre-election school assembly where all the candidates were to give their speeches. Mr. Everhart came up with a brilliant idea. "Reggie," he said, "what we can do is have you sit on Eddie's shoulder and throw an overcoat on you two. Eddie and you walk out on stage and you give your speech!"

Eddie was a classmate of mine. He had joined our class about halfway through the school year. He had previously dropped out of another school but had decided to go back. Everyone in school knew of Eddie because he was the tallest *kid* in the entire school, over 6 feet tall. I use the word kid, but to my schoolmates and me, he was not an ordinary school kid. While most of us were 12 or 13 years old, Eddie was about 17! No school bus for Eddie—he drove to school and parked in the teachers' parking lot!

Come assembly day, Eddie and I were ready! I had written a brief speech and practiced on Raynard for maybe a couple of weeks. Richard and I were the only candidates for vice president. He gave his speech first and got a nice round of applause. Meanwhile, Eddie and I were backstage trying to fight off the butterflies. I got on Eddie's shoulders and threw on Mr. Everhart's long gray overcoat. Mr. Everhart buttoned us up. Then I was introduced. With Eddie peeking out through the coat and holding onto my short legs, we slowly walked out on stage to the podium. To my amazement, the audience roared in laughter! They knew how short I was, so seeing me come out this tall was a funny sight. I must have stood more than 9 feet tall!

I do not recall any of my speech. My schoolmates probably did not remember what I said at the time, either, but they remembered my stunt and, on Election Day, the majority of them voted for me. I won by a landslide! Being that Richard was from a wealthy family, I got the anti-rich vote. I can still recall that I rushed home from Dunbar, and before I got down the hill to our house, I yelled to Mom, who was outside, "Momma, I won!" An on-again, off-again interest in politics had been born.

2

Pick 'em Up, Set 'em Down!
Welcome to the Air Force

⊷

On June 2, 1978, I graduated from Lexington Senior High School. Twenty-five days later, I left home to enter the United States Air Force. Mom had to sign me up because I was only 17 years old.

I left Lexington with mixed emotions. I was excited about leaving home because I had vowed not to go the route of so many Lexington Senior High School graduates: working in one of the many Lexington furniture factories. The factories seemed to offer grueling work, something I did not want to take on. Looking back, I think the administrators at our high school tried to steer the black and lower-class white students to the furniture factories and the middle- and upper-class white students to college. The fact that there were furniture factory owners sitting on the school board convinced me of this.

On the other hand, I was sad about leaving my family. The day I left was tough. Mom, along with my nephew Robbie and my friend Danny, drove me to Charlotte, where I was to be sworn in to the Air Force the next day. Before we departed Lexington, Mom drove me to the mattress factory where Raynard worked so we could say our goodbyes. What made this occasion even more somber was the fact that the factory was surrounded by a chain-link fence. He could not come outside the fence and we couldn't go inside, so my brother and I had to say our goodbyes while separated by the fence. Thankfully, that was not the last time we saw each other. That would have been an awful last moment with my twin brother.

At my hotel in Charlotte, I met my hotel roommate, another high school graduate who was joining the Air Force. I quickly unpacked and prepared to go out to dinner with my send-off crew, leaving my belongings in the room. Mom had to give me my one last life lesson before we parted ways: "Reggie," she said, "don't leave your valuables in your room with someone you have just met." My small-town naiveté had not escaped me just yet.

We had a nice dinner at a buffet restaurant, sharing a few memories and laughs at the table. Mom, Danny, and Robbie were proud of me for following through on my commitment. After dinner, we headed back to the hotel. We said our goodbyes without shedding tears, or at least I did—probably because my roommate was in the room. Mom reminded me to call her once I arrived in San Antonio.

The next day, my roommate and I were picked up and driven to the Armed Forces Center in downtown Charlotte. A couple of hundred young men and women from North Carolina and South Carolina were there to join the military. A group of us were assembled in a room. We were a rag-tag bunch, to say the least. There was no pomp in this room. Long hair, blue jeans, and t-shirts were the attire of the day. Nevertheless, there certainly was circumstance. We were told that we were about to be sworn in, and that once we took the oath, there was no turning back. As I raised my right hand, I had visions of my days in the Boy Scouts, saying the Scout Oath. I knew that this was no Scout outing, though. I did not back out of my commitment and was sworn in to the United States Air Force!

The Air Force immediately paid dividends for me. The trip from Charlotte to San Antonio was my very first flight!

Basic training was an eye opener. As soon as we got off the bus at Lackland Air Force Base, instructors began shouting: "Get in line!" "Set your bags down!" "Pick 'em up! Set 'em down!" They kept this up for a few minutes to ingrain in us right away that they were in charge. All the instructions and commands were mind-boggling. Thoughts of my Boy Scout days kept coming up, which was a good thing, because I think the Boy Scouts prepared me not just for leadership but for "followership."

Getting fitted for our uniforms was great. That was when I really started filling up with pride. I had not worn a uniform since I was in the Boy Scouts.

Despite all the yelling, I learned that the instructors, and all other Air Force personnel for that matter, could not lay a hand on us. So I figured I would let all the yelling and name calling go in one ear and out the other, and just do what I was told. Sometimes, the yelling actually got funny, especially since I knew that they could not hit us. To hear the instructors telling us young recruits that we were lower than whale manure was hilarious. You just couldn't let them see you smile; you might be instructed to write a hundred sentences saying something like, "I will not smile while being instructed by my technical instructor."

*

After about eight of the longest weeks of my life, we graduated basic training. Next on the schedule was technical training school at Keesler Air Force Base in Biloxi, Mississippi. Technical training school was where we would learn skills for the specific fields in which we would eventually work. My field was to be administration—an office job.

Technical training school was much closer to the real Air Force lifestyle than basic training. There was no more folding underwear, exercising, or curfews. But there was lots of partying and drinking. Keesler AFB had a nice and lively dance club. Eighteen was the drinking age, and that had come for me while I was in basic training. However, since I had gotten past the hardest part of the Air Force, basic training, and was now in school, I was not about to start a drinking binge like a few of the other basic training graduates. I kept my nose clean by not abusing my newfound freedom and went on to graduate from technical school after about six weeks.

In October 1978, as I was getting close to graduating from technical school, I received assignment orders to my permanent base, Little Rock Air Force Base in Jacksonville, Arkansas, a suburb of Little Rock. Little Rock AFB was home to more than eighty C-130 Hercules aircraft.

I was assigned a sponsor from the office where I was going to work. My sponsor wrote me a letter while I was still in Biloxi to fill me in on Little Rock and my upcoming job assignment. She informed me that I would be working in the 314th Field Maintenance Squadron, Jet Engine and Propeller Shop, as an administrative assistant. She also informed me that I would have two supervisors, Chief Master Sergeant Hobbs and Chief Master Sergeant Colvin. Chief master sergeant is the highest rank for a noncommissioned officer (NCO). Being assigned to two of these top dogs made me somewhat apprehensive about going to Little Rock.

Later that month, I flew to Little Rock AFB. Now this was

the real Air Force! This was where you basically forgot everything you learned in basic training and technical school and
did things the real Air Force way. But I still had to meet the
two top dogs.

When I arrived at the Jet Engine Shop, my sponsor introduced me to Chief Hobbs and Chief Colvin. Both men had
been in the Air Force for twenty years or more. Chief Hobbs,
the older of the two, was a white guy who drove an old pickup
truck and did a lot of hunting in Arkansas. He also had some
war stories to tell. Chief Colvin was black and had a son who
had just entered Air Force basic training.

My apprehension subsided very quickly because these
were two of the greatest gentlemen I would meet during my
seven-year Air Force career. I basically had two father figures
who looked out for me. What a way to start off my Air Force
career. Chief Colvin treated me like I was his son because his
own son was away. Chief Hobbs treated me like the son he
never had.

While in basic training, we had been taught about what
constitutes a professional and the meaning of professionalism,
as we were expected to become professionals. In the Jet Engine Shop, Chiefs Hobbs and Colvin exuded professionalism.
They both exemplified leadership, and everyone respected
them. On top of this, they were likeable guys. The other guys
loved to come into the office and shoot the breeze with them
and listen to Chief Hobbs' war stories. Both men also dressed
sharply in their uniforms, so I had to follow suit because I
wanted to come up to that measurement. Eventually, I wore a
necktie and Air Force cuff links to work. Some would say that
I was GQ in uniform.

I learned much from these two outstanding gentlemen. A
few of the lessons I learned included:
- Do the best you can with each task, be it large or small,
  important or not. This taught me to work at a high level

at all times, knowing that, pretty soon, that high level of output would become habitual.

- Do a great job whether someone sees you or not. In the Air Force, you develop a tendency to document your accomplishments so that when your annual performance report comes around, you have something glowing for your supervisor to write. However, the two chiefs instilled in me the understanding that while no one may see you do a particular job, someone will notice if you fail to do the job. The above is akin to initiative; doing a job without being told. The chiefs might not have recognized every time I performed a task, but they surely would remember the times they had to tell me to do a task. In a very short time, they realized I was getting my job done without being told.

- Learn your job thoroughly so that when you are called upon to do it in a hurry or under pressure, you will be prepared to do a professional job. In other words, do not panic. Over the years, I have learned from watching other people that when they panic, they lose focus and thereby lose their ability to do the best they can on a particular task.

As I mentioned, Little Rock AFB was the so-called real Air Force, where you could basically let your hair down. Working with Chiefs Hobbs and Colvin, though, I did not fully let my hair down; I could not do anything that would embarrass them. Moreover, I enjoyed the fact of being a professional at the young age of 18. Donning the Air Force uniform proudly, I felt great about being an airman and an American.

*

About a month after I arrived in Arkansas, state Attorney General William Jefferson Blythe Clinton was elected governor. Practically all I knew of him was that he was a young Democrat. At 32, he was the youngest person ever elected governor in Arkansas. Clinton would lose his re-election bid in 1980, but he would run again in 1982 and win. He would hold the office until his election as president in 1992.

I was not involved in politics at that time, especially Arkansas politics. I did not know much about the state, either. However, I soon found out that Arkansas' public education system was dismal, ranking forty-ninth or fiftieth among all the states in the country.

Little Rock was much larger than Lexington, but I found it to be a nice city. When other guys complained about Little Rock, I could not concur. Little Rock had a mall that we visited often, and there was a nice-size park downtown near Little Rock High School. This was the high school that Democratic Governor Orval Faubus and others did not want black students to attend in 1957. President Dwight Eisenhower, a Republican, had to call out the National Guard to provide protection so the "Little Rock Nine" could attend this school.

Visiting home for the first time from the Air Force was a proud moment for me. My family and friends thought highly of me for entering the Air Force. Occasionally, though, I did hear comments such as, "Reggie, you have changed. You act differently now that you are in the Air Force." Well, I hoped I had changed—for the better. After leaving home a 17-year-old high school graduate, I hoped that I had matured after all I had been through in basic training, technical school, and about six months at Little Rock AFB, all out from under Mom's roof.

One of the more interesting things that went on at Little Rock AFB was an Air Force training program for the Iranian military. There was a handful of Iranian military troops being trained to repair jet engines and working in other shops in the 314th Field Maintenance Squadron. Of course, that all changed sometime after November 4, 1979, when fifty-two Americans were taken hostage in Tehran, Iran.

A more amusing moment came when the media was duped by the Air Force. The Strategic Airlift Command (SAC) maintained missile silos in Arkansas. When a minor missile accident occurred at one of the silos, the news media came out and wanted to investigate what had happened and what we were going to do about repairing the missile. The news showed what was reported to be the damaged missile warhead being towed to a repair shop. Being that I worked in the Jet Engine Shop, I laughed when I saw an engine can, a container that housed C-130 jet engines, being towed down the street rather than a missile warhead!

You meet a lot of interesting people in the military. One such person was Brindsley Clyde Ward, who was my room dog. He hailed from Trinidad. I became great friends with him and with the other Trinidadians at Little Rock AFB. They introduced us Americans to reggae music, including Bob Marley and Peter Tosh. (Strangely, the Trinidadians and other foreigners did not have to become United States citizens to join the U.S. military.)

Brindsley was an airman who marched to his own beat. He was a C-130 jet engine mechanic who got to know that engine inside and out. Chief Hobbs looked out for him because he respected Brindsley's talent with a wrench and safety wire. So when Brindsley caught some flak for somehow having hair that was an inch long during roll call, meeting the hair-length guidelines during roll call and then somehow having a 10-inch afro on the weekends, or for his propensity for being late, Chief Hobbs instructed Brindsley's supervisor to cut him some slack.

Serving in the military somewhat secluded me from some of the things that other military personnel and civilians had to go through. Because I was single and lived in the dormitory, inflation did not affect me much. Still, I remember well that under President Jimmy Carter inflation increasingly had a negative effect on the country. Interest rates on credit cards and mortgages shot up under Carter, a fact that some Democrats would like us to forget.

As I mentioned earlier, I was not engaged in politics while in Little Rock. My mom was a big President Carter supporter, and I respected him as our commander-in-chief. But I must say I lost some respect for him during his re-election campaign. At one point, he was trailing Ronald Reagan in the polls. The news media was causing people to be somewhat apprehensive about Reagan, suggesting that if Reagan won, he would start World War III with his "itchy trigger finger." Some people liked this about him; he seemed very supportive of the military. By contrast, Carter was looking weak militarily, especially after the disastrous attempt to rescue the American hostages in Iran. So Carter decided to let the cat out of the bag about a stealth bomber that the Air Force had in the works. This did not sit well with me, along with a quite a few other Americans, especially in our military.

Reagan went on to win and the hostages were released on Inauguration Day, January 20, 1981.

3

Washington, D.C., and the Air Force One Presidential Wing

———◆———

My initial career plans were to stay in the Air Force for four years, learn a trade, then get out and move back to Lexington. At least that was what I told my supervisor at the A&P grocery store in Lexington before I joined the military. Those plans changed somewhat in 1981, when my best friend, Steve Ferguson, got a special-duty assignment to Andrews Air Force Base with the 89th Military Airlift Wing, Air Force One Presidential Wing. Steve is from Baltimore, Maryland, so going to Andrews AFB in suburban Washington, D.C., was like going home to him. He told me how nice Andrews AFB and D.C. were, making it sound so exciting. Eventually, he talked me into trying to get stationed there.

However, being assigned to the Air Force One Presidential Wing would mean a change in my career plans. To get the assignment, I would have to be discharged, ending my current four-year enlistment, and then re-enlist for four additional years. This procedure is used with most special-duty assignments to minimize turnover of personnel.

To be assigned to the Presidential Wing, you must have a stellar background and an unblemished record. Under the guidance of my two father figures, Chiefs Hobbs and Colvin, I had kept my nose clean, and my annual performance reports were beyond reproach. To apply, I had to put together a package that included those performance reports, plus recommendation letters and a full-length photo of me in uniform. I also included documents showing that I had been promoted early (below-the-zone) to senior airman and had been selected Airman of the Month of Little Rock Air Force Base in October 1979 in recognition of superior performance.

I contacted my family back home to let them know that I was trying to get assigned to the Presidential Wing. President Reagan had replaced President Carter in January 1981, and I wasn't sure how Mom would feel about me trying to go work with a Republican president. I hoped she would think I was doing something right in my Air Force career by just applying.

Lo and behold, I was accepted! Not only was I leaving Little Rock, I was heading to our nation's capital. Going back to the East Coast, I would be closer to North Carolina and to Richmond, Virginia, where Dad lived. He had been a long-time employee with tobacco giant Philip Morris.

I had to be at Andrews AFB by December 31, 1981. Having never visited our nation's capital, I decided to arrive on New Year's Eve to bring in the New Year on a high note. My Air Force buddy, Gerard, rode along with me to North Carolina so he could head home to Annapolis, Maryland, for the holidays.

We departed Little Rock AFB on December 12. After spending a few days of leave in Lexington with my family, I drove to Richmond to spend time with Dad.

While in Richmond, we located Truck and Linda, a married couple who were friends of mine at Little Rock and who now lived in Richmond. Linda somewhat filled me in on D.C. She told me it was a "fast" city and you had to be careful. I had never thought about how fast D.C. would be, considering that practically every city was faster than Lexington. Nevertheless, I took heed of her words—I think.

On December 31, I departed Richmond for Washington, D.C., about a two-hour drive. I arrived at Andrews AFB early in the evening. After getting a temporary room, I drove to the base Noncommissioned Officer (NCO) Club to find out where the party was; after all, it was New Year's Eve. I immediately met a guy who told me about a nightclub off base called the Quonset Hut. When I got there, the Quonset Hut was jumping! I thought back to what Linda had told me and said to myself that this must be what she had meant by "fast." Being 21 years old and single, from that night on until I left D.C. four years later, the party was on!

*

D.C. was not all partying, fun, and games, though. During my time in D.C., I experienced the highest of highs and the lowest of lows, not only personally but professionally, as well.

On January 13, 1982, after I had been at Andrews AFB only two weeks, it snowed so heavily that we got off work early. I was well acclimated to winter weather; both Lexington and Little Rock get snow. But snow in D.C. was quite different. It seemed much thicker and colder than that to which I was accustomed.

When my buddies and I got to our dormitory, we turned on the television and saw the breaking news about a plane crash. It was Air Florida's Flight 90, which had crashed into the Potomac River in D.C. After realizing that this was live on television in our own city, we sat and watched in amazement. We saw a woman struggling in the Potomac River, where the plane had broken through the ice. The woman appeared to be a blind passenger. She had a helpless and blank look in her eyes as she kept coming up above the water and then, after a brief struggle, going back under. We later found out that she was a flight attendant who was in shock. One bystander was on the bank of the river, watching her desperately cling to life. Suddenly, he courageously jumped into the water and saved her.

At another location in the river, several passengers from the plane, both men and women, were trying to hang on to be rescued. One of the passengers was Arland D. Williams, Jr. When a rescue helicopter came and lowered a life ring, Mr. Williams took charge to help everyone get in the life ring one at a time. At one point, when he was trying to help a woman get to the life ring, another man grabbed it for himself, completely overlooking the women who were still in the water. My friends and I were absolutely furious at this man who put himself ahead of the women. But Mr. Williams did not seem to try to take the life ring from this selfish man; he simply let the man be hoisted up by the helicopter. Everyone at that location was eventually rescued except the hero, Mr. Williams. He seemed to run out of energy after he got the last person rescued.

The selfish man was later interviewed on television while in his hospital bed. He told the news crew that he tried to help the other people get out of the water. I could not believe it! His version of things didn't match what I saw on television. To this day, I think that if the guys in the water had worked together, Mr. Williams could have been rescued too.

Later, during the recovery of the bodies and the airplane, my unit, the Aerospace Ground Equipment (AGE) Shop, sent personnel and equipment, such as lights and heaters that are used for Air Force One and the other Andrews AFB aircraft, to the crash site. My squadron's participation was greatly appreciated because this was a very cold operation and the heaters helped warm the tents used by the rescue and recovery crew.

All the rescue and recovery agencies did an outstanding job during this emergency. The individual heroes, such as Arland D. Williams, Jr., were just phenomenal and showed everyone what it means to put others' lives before your own and perform the ultimate sacrifice.

*

Once the weather warmed up that year, I began to tour D.C. Driving around the capital is no fun, though, when you do not know your way around. With all the one-way streets, diagonal streets, roundabouts, and enormous potholes, learning the streets of D.C. is like learning the Rubik's Cube. On top of that, the stoplights can be confusing. On one block, you may be driving in Maryland, where the stoplights are above the intersections. On the next block, you can be in D.C., where the stoplights are on poles on the side of the street. I can't tell you how many red lights I ran or how many one-way streets I went down the wrong way while feeling my way around our nation's capital.

Eventually, I got smart and purchased a ten-speed bicycle. There is no better way to crack the Rubik's Cube of D.C.'s streets than by touring around on a bicycle. I rode to practically every museum, monument, historical statue, and neighborhood D.C. had to offer. I rode to Watergate and discovered that the Watergate scandal was named after a hotel. Foggy Bottom, which is the State Department, was also interesting.

All this riding around could sometimes get tiring, and I would need to take a nap. Knowing how D.C. could be dangerous with the number of criminals there, I napped with a fish filleting knife hidden by my side, just in case I had to fight off a bad guy. My favorite place to take a break was in Georgetown. As I recall, there is a little art gallery on M Street. Out the back door of the gallery is a little backyard garden park, which was great for napping.

With all the riding I did, I began to learn my way around. Our nation's capital is divided into four sections: NE, SE, NW, and SW, with each having its own numbered streets—1st, 2nd, 3rd, and so forth—as well as alphabet streets—A, B, C, and so forth—that do not necessarily extend over to the other sections. Streets that run diagonal are named after states. Then there are streets named after trees. At last, I cracked the Rubik's Cube of D.C.!

*

On February 18, 1983, while I was at work in the AGE Shop, Dad called me. He was crying. He said, "Reggie, Raynard is dead." I was devastated and heartbroken. I could not believe it. Dad told me that Raynard had died in his sleep; the cause was later diagnosed as heart failure. I told Dad that I would meet him at his house in Richmond.

After gathering some composure, I told my supervisor, Senior Master Sergeant Craig, the awful news. He asked my coworker and friend, Staff Sergeant Gerald Joyner, to drive me to my dormitory. After getting my things together, I drove to Richmond, seemingly crying half the way there. Once I got to Dad's house, we cried in each other's arms. We finally got ourselves together and made the trek to Lexington. On the way, we kept our spirits up somewhat by talking about the good times we had with Raynard.

Nard was not exactly a Momma's boy, but he really cared about her. He was the last of the siblings to leave home. He unselfishly hung around so she wouldn't be by herself and succumb to the empty-nest syndrome. He eventually moved to Atlanta to live with Michael and his wife, Anita. He died in their home at the age of 22.

Arriving home at Mom's house was even sadder. Mom had a house full of people. I immediately rushed to her and we embraced, with me crying like a baby. Even now, tears well up in my eyes as I recall this sad time and write about it.

I am saddened that my son, Reginald, and daughter, Taylor, never got to meet Raynard. They certainly know of him, even though I rarely talk about him. It's too sad for me to talk about him, I guess. However, we do visit his gravesite at our old "sports field" every time we go to Lexington.

*

Working with SMSgt Craig in the AGE Shop office was rewarding. We did have one slight problem, though; our musical tastes were quite different. I enjoyed R&B music stations on the radio. SMSgt Craig liked bluegrass music. Thinking back, I am not sure how he found a bluegrass music station in D.C.; it must have been broadcast out of West Virginia. Being a nice guy, SMSgt Craig decided to compromise; he tuned the radio to WTOP, an all-news station on the AM dial. Although I had grown up reading the *Lexington Dispatch* newspaper, and while in Little Rock I had perused the two rival newspapers, listening to WTOP really got me interested in current events and the political scene of D.C. I became a news junkie. There's no better place to follow news and politics than our nation's capital.

I even started reading the *Washington Post* newspaper, but it was only years later that I learned of its politically left-leaning slant. Neither was I astute enough to see through some of its "news" stories, such as the one about the Reagan administration wanting ketchup to count as a vegetable in school cafeterias. Still, this was one story that I found hard to swallow (pun intended).

I was not politically active at this time. I was around the age of 22 or 23, and I still had not cast my first vote in an election. However, I did have much respect and admiration for President Reagan. He had been instrumental in getting our hostages released from Iran on his Inauguration Day. And he had restored dignity to the military and boosted our morale merely by showing us respect after some dismal years under President Carter. Plus, John Hinckley had attempted to assassinate Reagan before I arrived in D.C., so I felt sorry for him and even more so for his press secretary, James Brady, who was shot and paralyzed. On top of all of this, first and foremost, he was my commander-in-chief and I was working with the Air Force One Presidential Wing, of which I was proud to be a member. Not many people could look out the back doors of their offices and see the president departing or arriving on Air Force One, the most respected aircraft in the world.

Shortly after being promoted to staff sergeant in the fall of 1983, I was selected to attend the Noncommissioned Officer Leadership School at Dover Air Force Base in Dover, Delaware. I found Dover to be a nice place to attend school. Delaware State, a black college, is located there, and its library was a great place to study, as well as to meet Delaware State students.

The Leadership School lasted a month, but I was there for only about a week or so before I learned up close about one of the other missions of Dover AFB—carrying out forensics on our fallen service members.

In Beirut, Lebanon, on October 23, 1983, someone drove a truck filled with explosives up to a U.S. military barracks and detonated it, eventually killing 241 Marine, Navy, and Army service members. Days after the bombing, the bodies were flown to Dover AFB. The community must have been accustomed to service members arriving in body bags at Dover AFB, but seeing 241 bodies arrive at one time left the whole base somber. As the national news media descended upon Dover, the base put on a ceremony that my classmates and I attended. It was a sad time for us, and the deaths and the ceremony put a new perspective on the Leadership School.

Coming from the Air Force One Presidential Wing, I felt that I had to do well in the class. The students who finished in the top 10 percent of the Leadership School would be designated as Distinguished Graduates. I set a goal to be in that top 10 percent. My classmates rarely saw me after class because I headed to Delaware State's library to study and do homework, as well as meet some of the college females, killing two birds with one stone.

On graduation night, November 22, 1983, there were guests from our wings, squadrons, and units in attendance. My squadron sent a lower-ranking individual as its representative. This left me somewhat disappointed. I thought that if I could earn Distinguished Graduate honors, my squadron might feel embarrassed about sending a low-ranking representative.

The names of the students in the top 10 percent were to be announced during the ceremony. None of us students knew how we had fared in our grading, so we did not know who was in the top 10 percent. As the names were being called, I sat patiently, hoping my name would be called. Sure enough, it was! I walked up to join my fellow Distinguished Graduates. My squadron's representative and I were elated.

The good news got back to Andrews AFB before I did. When I arrived, my office co-workers congratulated me for doing an outstanding job in school and representing the Air Force One Presidential Wing.

*

Arlington National Cemetery, located in metro Washington, D.C., is considered America's most hallowed ground. War heroes, astronauts, presidents, and other famous people have been laid to rest in this cemetery. But there are some buried there who are not famous or war heroes. An Air Force servicewoman named Melanie, whose last name escapes me, is one of them.

Arlington was not on my list of places to visit in D.C. I respected the cemetery for all it represented, but I had no plans to visit it—not until after Melanie's tragic death. Melanie and her husband, Gary, were expecting their first child. Gary was also in the Air Force One Presidential Wing. During the delivery of their baby at Malcolm Grow Medical Center, the base hospital, Melanie experienced complications. The baby eventually was born in good condition. But Melanie died soon after giving birth. We soon found out that the hospital staff had made some grave errors during the delivery.

The sad news hit our squadron very hard. All of us knew both Melanie and Gary, and knowing how much they loved one another, we knew Melanie's death would be a tremendous loss for Gary. We all tried to do what we could to comfort and console him. He had to deal not just with his loss but with his anger over the mistakes that had caused Melanie's death.

On a bright sunny day, a group of us rode together to Arlington National Cemetery for the funeral. It was a quiet ride. I do not think that any of us had ever been there. Riding through the cemetery, I was truly in awe of the size of the grounds and the sheer number of white crosses. With all the roads running throughout the grounds, one could get lost there. The graveyard that I played in as a boy in Lexington was no match for Arlington National Cemetery.

Riding through the grounds conjured up many thoughts.

The vastness, peacefulness, and rolling hills reminded me of the countryside. Seeing all the crosses also made me think about the wars that most of the dead in Arlington had served in versus the Cold War in which I was serving. Thinking about the service of these fallen men and women made my service seem somewhat meaningless, even if I was serving with the Air Force One Presidential Wing. Most of these men and women had served without a lot of fanfare, without the pomp and circumstance to which I had become accustomed. Then, with the number of crosses in the cemetery, I thought about the many people that each death had affected, like our procession of family and friends. I calculated the age of some of the fallen and saw there were many who had not reached the age of 21.

After going up and down hills, turning here and turning there, we finally arrived at our destination—Melanie's burial site. The family and friends gathered around as the honor guard performed their duties. They folded the U.S. flag and presented it to Gary. A twenty-one-gun salute was given, with the shots echoing out through the cemetery. It was a sad day for the Air Force, but an even sadder day for Melanie's family and friends.

While riding back through Arlington National Cemetery, passing all the crosses again, I selfishly tried to uplift my service to the country, comparing my service to that of the fallen. I thought back to basic training, when I learned the word *deterrence*. We were taught that the U.S. military's weaponry and personnel, along with the threat to use that weaponry and personnel, served as a deterrent to our Cold War enemies. We were saying to our enemies, "If you attack us, we are going to retaliate with such a devastating blow that you will wish you had never been born." Thinking about the word *deterrence* got me thinking about another word—*prevention*. I told myself that we were serving to prevent another Arlington National

Cemetery. Still, there was no comparison between my service and that of those who had died, because they had paid the ultimate sacrifice.

*

While at Andrews AFB, I joined a dance show called "The Dance Connection" that was filmed at Howard University. From that, I became a runway model and eventually formed a modeling troupe at Andrews AFB.

One weekend, my brother Mike came to visit me. Mike is a photographer, so he came up to do a photo shoot of me. During Mike's visit, Andrews AFB put on an air show. I surprised Mike by saying, "Let's go over to one of the hangars to check out some airplanes." When we got near the hangar, he was surprised to see all the airplanes for the air show. It was Mike's first air show, and he thoroughly enjoyed it.

One memorable time for me was in late June 1985, when Dad drove up from Richmond to hang out with me for a few days. It was his first time at Andrews AFB, so I decided to give him the grand tour of the base and my workplace.

Earlier in the month, TWA Flight 847 had departed Athens, Greece, en route to Rome, Italy, with numerous Americans on board. The plane had been hijacked by three Hezbollah Shi'ite terrorists. U.S. Navy diver Petty Officer Robert Stethem had been beaten and eventually shot to death.

After much negotiation, thirty-nine American hostages were finally freed on June 30. On July 2, they were flown to Andrews AFB. My Dad and I, along with others, walked out to the flight line to greet them. President Reagan attended also and delivered a speech. Taking Dad out to see the hostages and the president was a thrill for me.

Later in Dad's visit, he told me that he was proud of me and my assignment to the Air Force One Presidential Wing. I had always known that Dad was proud of me and my military accomplishments, but hearing him tell me that really meant the world to me.

As time went on, my admiration for President Reagan grew, mostly because of his stance against communism. When Reagan won re-election, I volunteered to be in the Inaugural Parade on January 21, 1985. The other Air Force volunteers and I assembled at Andrews AFB in the frigid cold weather, all dressed up in our winter attire, only to be told later that the parade had been cancelled because it was too cold.

*

I venture to say that my peers and I, or America in general, had never heard of the Contras or the Sandinistas until President Reagan brought them to the attention of America. I quickly learned that the Sandinistas in Nicaragua were pro-communist, supported by the Soviet Union, and the Contras were anti-communist rebels. Reagan wanted to help the Contras to prevent the Soviet Union from establishing a beachhead in our hemisphere.

The Iran-Contra saga helped forge my belief in Reagan and his stance against communism. I was disappointed in the way the Democrats tried to thwart Reagan from preventing communism from gaining a significant beachhead in the Americas. The Democrats' confrontations with Reagan and the Republicans about fighting back against communism caused me to wonder whether the Democrats were putting their dislike of Republicans over their dislike of our enemy. Even today, I wonder whether Democrats are putting their dislike of President Bush over their dislike of terrorists.

I have been in debates with others who say that Republican sycophants tried to run President Clinton out of town for breaking the law, just as Democrats tried to do with Reagan. The clear difference is that Reagan and his administration were accused of breaking the law to fight communism while Clinton and company were accused of breaking the law to cover up sexual peccadilloes and lying under oath.

*

In November 1985, my final month in the Air Force, I was given a going-away party at my office. My co-workers presented me a silver pen and pencil set that I have since lost, and most notably, an Air Force Commendation Medal (First Oak Leaf Cluster) for meritorious service. I also received a photograph of Air Force One that had been autographed by presidential pilot Colonel Robert Ruddick. Fortunately, I had an extra copy of the Air Force One photo because the autographed photo was damaged beyond repair by water a few years later.

I ended my Air Force career after a little more than seven years of duty, being honorably discharged. My last day on Andrews Air Force Base was low-key and unassuming, at least on the surface. I drove through the gate in my 1976 Volvo alone, heading to Richmond to visit Dad. I had had a stellar career with only a few incidents. Being in the Air Force for that length of time and accomplishing the things I had made me feel good about myself. Having gone from a small-town, 17-year-old boy to being honorably discharged after working with the Air Force One Presidential Wing was something that I knew would be a tremendous highlight of my life.

4

Welcome to Hotlanta

⸺◆⸺

After my honorable discharge from the Air Force, I headed south to Hotlanta, as the Atlantans called it. After brief stops in Richmond and Lexington, I went on to Atlanta to work with my brother Michael and his wife, Anita. Michael was an executive with the Boy Scouts of America and Anita was an executive with a temporary-service company. But in between camping and sending out temps on job assignments, they had found time to start a family business, Bohannon Enterprises Inc.

Bohannon Enterprises started out in the photography, modeling, and jewelry businesses. After more than twenty years in business, the company, now named Bovanti, has expanded the photography and modeling businesses, and has added Bovanti Spa and Bovanti Cosmetics, which is the main focus of the company.

Bovanti is truly a family business. Michael and Anita's

daughters, Marquis and Marquel, grew up working in the business. My own children, Reginald and Taylor, have put in their time, as well. And since arriving in Atlanta in November 1985, I have worked with Bovanti both full- and part-time. Like the majority of businesses, Bovanti has had its up and down days (though far more ups than downs). Even relationships sometimes get strained. That is why I work on a part-time basis—to keep my familial relationship with Michael intact.

Leaving the Air Force and moving to another city was a fairly smooth transition for me. I latched onto the television news and newspapers of Atlanta. At the time, Atlanta had two main newspapers—the *Atlanta Constitution* and the *Atlanta Journal*. Unfortunately for the city, the more liberal Constitution bought out the more conservative Journal. The city's paper is now called the *Atlanta Journal-Constitution*.

It took me only a short while after arriving in Atlanta to get back into the habit of listening to news radio. Sadly, I discovered WGST-AM on a tragic day. While scanning radio stations on the morning of January 28, 1986, I found WGST reporting the Challenger space shuttle explosion. From what I recall, Neal Boortz was on the air at the time. Since that day, I have been a listener of WGST and of Boortz, who has since moved to WSB-AM.

Listening to Boortz was my first exposure to talk radio, and it was quite an education. One of the first things I learned was that I was not going to agree with everything he or any other talk show host or commentator said or thought. He advises his listeners to have several news sources. Once you have several sources, you can weigh all the facts and opinions that you absorb, then develop your own opinions and beliefs about a particular topic.

Anita signed me up with her temporary agency and soon began sending me out on assignments. One long-term assignment was with the Federal Aviation Administration's Southern Region Office near Hartsfield-Jackson International Airport. During the time that I worked with the FAA, I turned my supervisor on to Boortz, the self-appointed "High Priest of the Church of the Painful Truth." Neither of us was accustomed to someone discussing taboo topics, especially racial issues, on the radio, as Boortz did. So there were a few times we wanted to call in and give him a piece of our minds. We held back from calling, though, and just continued to listen. After getting over the shock of Boortz's points of view and dropping my feelings that he was a racist, I began to like him.

WGST also had a two-man show with Tom Houck, a liberal, and Dick Williams, a conservative. They were quite entertaining, as well as informative. They constantly had debates on political issues. Their show was a great window to the liberal and conservative mindsets and how the two sides couched issues.

One day in 1988, from what I recall, WGST decided to join the *Rush Limbaugh Show* in progress. For me, hearing Limbaugh's show was akin to culture shock. There were rapid-fire topics and comments of a type that had rarely been voiced before in a national forum. Here was a man hammering Democratic politicians and their beliefs. He was also denigrating the liberal mainstream media, something I, along with millions of others, had never heard before.

One of the biggest lessons I learned from Limbaugh was the fact that most media outlets are liberal and Democrat leaning. Initially, I found this hard to fathom. But Rush doesn't just say that ABC, CBS, NBC, CNN, NPR, and some others are liberal media outlets. He doesn't just opine about most newspapers, including the *New York Times*, the *Washington Post*, the *Los Angeles Times*, and the *Atlanta Journal-Constitution*, being pro-Democrat. Rush supports these statements with proof. He is forever playing comments that aired on these networks or reading articles from these papers to prove what he says. And this is what really gets to the Rush haters. Pre-Rush, these media outlets were able to broadcast and print their liberal slant because they did not have much neutral or, for that matter, conservative competition.

For a long time, the liberal media outlets tried to dismiss Rush as a buffoon and a flash in the pan. They even criticized and made fun of his audience, as if it would make his listeners go away. Fat chance!

Another important fact that Rush points out is that liberal politicians are afraid to admit that they actually are liberals. For the most part, that is because they have an agenda that is somewhat hidden, and they know that if the American people truly knew what they were up to, we would not support them. And what really gets the liberal politicians is that Rush points this out on a daily basis, using their own comments, statements, and speeches.

Having been a student of the "Limbaugh Institute for Advanced Conservative Studies" since 1988, I recommend that others enroll, especially blacks. Rather than listening as liberals give their wrongheaded opinions and distortions of Rush in an effort to turn blacks and other minorities away from his school, I recommend that everyone get an education from Professor Limbaugh himself!

After Boortz moved to WSB, Sean Hannity joined WGST. Hannity was (and is) a great talk show talent with strong conservative beliefs. He, too, was a student of Limbaugh.

During the 1988 presidential election campaign, the Democratic Party decided to hold its convention in Atlanta. I was almost three years removed from the Air Force. Having never voted before, I figured this would be a great time to get involved in politics.

Jesse Jackson threw his hat into the presidential race, so I decided to volunteer to work with his campaign committee. I signed up in early 1988. I was really looking forward to volunteering once the convention came to town. I was 27 years old at the time and was quite eager to work with Jackson. Mom must have been proud of me, for I was following in her footsteps by working on a Democratic candidate's campaign.

During the run-up to the convention, Jackson worked at a frenetic pace via the Rainbow Coalition, registering people to vote. Jackson and the Rainbow Coalition brought a lot of enthusiasm to the campaign. First-time registrants and veteran voters were energized to get out, campaign, and hopefully vote for Jackson.

For my volunteer efforts during the Super Tuesday primaries, I received a Certificate of Appreciation, albeit a few months late. The certificate was dated March 10, 1988, and the accompanying letter was dated June 10, 1988. The letter from Eugene Walker, chairman of the Jesse Jackson Georgia Committee, stated that, "The Atlanta office was closed, and the postage funds dried up."

The Democrats had several potential presidential nominees that year. In addition to Jackson, candidates included Michael Dukakis, Bruce Babbitt, Joe Biden, Dick Gephardt, Al Gore, Gary Hart, and the late Paul Simon. They vied throughout the winter and spring to be their party's pick. But by the time they arrived in Atlanta, Dukakis had risen above the field.

The minorities of America, particularly blacks, were excited about having representation in the presidential race. Even black female Lenora Fulani of the New Alliance Party got into the race. She became the first black and female to get on the ballots of all fifty states.

The city of Atlanta was bursting with pride over being selected as the host city for the Democratic Convention. Downtown Atlanta went through an extensive makeover. The now-demolished Omni Arena was given an interior overhaul to accommodate the convention. Mayor Andrew Young and the powers-that-be took this opportunity to improve the city's infrastructure by repairing roads and Interstate 75/85, which runs through downtown. There were so many orange construction cones on the streets and highways of downtown Atlanta that some national media outlets—Northern outlets, no doubt—questioned whether the city would be ready and able to handle the convention.

Eventually, Atlanta was indeed ready and eager to show off some Southern hospitality. On July 18, 1988, the Omni Arena flung its doors open to the conventioneers.

Jackson and the Rainbow Coalition came to Atlanta fully represented and ready for a historic occasion. I felt that if Jackson would not be nominated as the presidential nominee, certainly he would be the vice-presidential running mate; after all, the Democratic Party was the party of minorities.

Each night, July 18-21, the delegates and media representatives filled the Omni Arena to its capacity and beyond. The crowds were so large, the Atlanta fire marshal closed down the turnstiles, locking out delegates and the media. Even Bill Nigut, a popular local liberal-leaning political reporter, was denied access to the party on the convention's most important night. "Do you know who I am?" did not work for him that night.

As much as I would have liked to have been there, I did not get into the convention on any night, though I did join the party outside the Omni Arena. Someone said it was like being at a Grateful Dead concert because of all the characters out there in the parking lot. I collected several souvenirs—buttons, bumper stickers, and the like—for Mom and me. After soaking in the festivities, I went home to watch the convention on television. I recall Ann Richards, who was then the governor of Texas, getting the crowd fired up with her keynote address. She was an instant hit when she said, speaking of Vice President George H.W. Bush, the Republican nominee: "Poor

George. He can't help it. He was born with a silver spoon in his mouth."

The sexual escapades of actor Rob Lowe made the convention even wackier. The local news got hold of a videotape of him having sex with two females, one of whom was under age. That followed the sexual scandal that had derailed Hart's campaign some months before. That Democratic presidential campaign was one active race.

Then there was Jackson. He delivered a fine and inspirational speech—at least that is what I thought at the time. I recently decided to review his speech and see exactly what made it so fine and inspirational, and to see its relevance today. The first thing that popped out at me about his speech was his use of the term *common ground*. It epitomized some Democrats' way of thinking; they act as if there should be no rich or poor people—they want everyone in the same boat, regardless of the choices that the rich, poor, or anyone else make in their lives.

Eventually, the delegates nominated Dukakis as their presidential candidate to run against Bush. I was not necessarily pleased with Dukakis winning the nomination, but I could not complain.

I was still hoping that, with all the efforts of Jackson and the Rainbow Coalition, that Jackson would be chosen as the Democrats' vice presidential candidate. After all, the Democratic Party is the party of blacks, right? Don't more than 90 percent of blacks vote for the Democratic Party? But the vice presidential candidate is chosen by the presidential nominee and his staff, and to my disappointment, the Democrats selected Texas Senator Lloyd Bentsen.

I was truly disgusted with these running mate shenanigans. I can look back and see that the Democratic Party's vice-presidential choice for the 1988 election was the beginning of my disgruntlement with the party. Regardless, I cast my first-ever presidential vote for Dukakis.

*

During the 1992 presidential election campaign, Limbaugh pointed out several issues about Bill Clinton, things that the mainstream media did not touch on. He mainly focused on Clinton's character, or lack thereof. He also harped on the fact that Clinton's sycophants kept up the mantra that character did not matter. And he brought out how Clinton loathed the military. That did not sit too well with this veteran, but being a Democrat, I overlooked this minor point.

Limbaugh talked about and played tapes that Gennifer Flowers had secretly made of herself and Clinton. On the tapes, they discussed sex, as well as New York Governor Mario Cuomo, with Clinton saying Cuomo "acts like" a Mafiaso. But even knowing all of this negative and derogatory information about Clinton, I cast my presidential vote for him. After all, I am black and Mom is a Democrat.

In my heart, I wanted to vote for President George H.W. Bush, particularly since he had been my deputy commander-in-chief when I had worked with the Air Force One Presidential Wing. Perhaps the fact that President Bush did not know the price of milk at the grocery store persuaded me, but I didnt think about the fact that no president—Bush, Clinton, or any other—goes shopping for groceries.

5

The Heart of a Patriot

O ver the years, I have come to love my country deep- ly. Being a Boy Scout and then later joining the Air Force had a strong impact on me that helped to instill patrio- tism in me.

We the People of the United States, in Order to form a more perfect Union, establish Justice, insure domestic Tranquility, provide for the common defence, promote the general Welfare, and secure the Blessings of Liberty to ourselves and our Pos- terity, do ordain and establish this Constitution for the United States of America.

The words above, which constitute the preamble to the United States Constitution, were penned in 1787 by Gou- verneur Morris of New York, a delegate to the Constitutional Convention in Philadelphia, Pennsylvania. Here is a meaning- ful introduction to the greatest legal document ever written:

More than a hundred countries have modeled their constitutions after it.

Neal Boortz used to talk about the Constitution quite often. He would discuss how Americans had become accustomed to rights that are not even in the Constitution and how our politicians, Republicans and Democrats alike, have led us and the country far from the meaning of the founders. Boortz talked about words that are not in the Constitution, such as *democracy* and *education*.

All these discussions on the Constitution began to intrigue me, particularly when Boortz talked about how black people came to be considered three-fifths of a person. Discussions about how this came about and how it benefited blacks caused me to think I needed to read this Constitution that he talked about so much.

What I discovered first about the Constitution was that there is not much to it, insofar as length and content. It has a preamble, seven articles, and twenty-seven amendments, and that is basically it. Pitifully, the only thing that I could recall learning about the Constitution in school was the preamble and a little bit about the Bill of Rights. I knew very little about what was in the articles. As a matter of fact, I did not know the Constitution had articles!

For further learning about the Constitution, I turned to the Federalist Papers. I purchased a book of the eighty-five essays and downloaded a searchable text file. The Federalist Papers are where you find an in-depth understanding of what the Founding Fathers had in mind when the Constitution was written. Alexander Hamilton, James Madison, and John Jay wrote the essays and published them anonymously under the name *Publius*. I found the Federalist Papers to be great winter reading.

Being that I am black, I took an in-depth look at how the Constitution pertains to blacks as a race. I purchased a book titled *Slavery and The Founders—Race and Liberty in the Age of Jefferson*, by Paul Finkelman. It discusses articles and sections of the Constitution that excluded blacks or just did not apply to them. Over time, though, these inequities have become moot or have been corrected. People like Justice Thurgood Marshall and attorneys John Scott, Jack Greenburg, and Louis C. Redding held America's feet to the fire by fighting for the right for the Constitution to apply to all Americans. The 13th, 14th, 15^{th,} and 24th Amendments were written specifically to rectify racial wrongs in the Constitution. Now I feel that we blacks have to vigilantly make sure that whatever rights are enumerated in the Constitution serve us as well as other Americans. When we blacks, or any other group or segment for that matter, demand constitutional rights exclusively for ourselves, it dilutes the Constitution and makes it difficult to view it as a manual that should apply to all Americans. Simply put, if it applies to one, it should apply to all.

Thanks to Boortz, I am pleased to say that I have learned a great deal about our Constitution. I know what each of the seven articles and all twenty-seven amendments pertain to! I can even recite a few of the amendments word for word. I am a Constitution enthusiast and would even consider myself a Constitution scholar, at least compared to the so-called Constitution scholars who popped up everywhere during President Clinton's impeachment saga. My level of knowledge and understanding was superior to that of quite a few of them. Of course, it's possible that they were just pulling the wool over the majority of Americans' eyes, knowing that only a handful of us have even read the Constitution.

Regarding Clinton's impeachment, after all was said and done, I felt that both he and Congress, including the Senate, ran roughshod over our Constitution, especially Clinton. To raise your right hand and say that you will protect and defend the Constitution, only to be taken to court for lying to one of the branches of government that the Constitution established, the judiciary, is disgraceful.

I did not lose my enthusiasm for the Constitution during this sad time. But I look at it somewhat differently now. I now see the Constitution as a document with a great past that has been diluted and overlooked by the very people who are supposed to uphold it—the politicians.

*

Once I became a Constitution enthusiast, I naturally had to share my enthusiasm and knowledge with my kids, Reggie and Taylor. Knowing that they would soon be studying the Constitution in school, I decided to teach them the preamble beforehand. I also read constitutional current-events articles to them so they could get an understanding of how the Constitution relates to them today.

In 2000, when Reggie was in the fourth grade, he told his teacher, Ms. Hoskins, about all the books I had about the Constitution. He told her that I knew a lot about it. Later, she asked me if I could speak to her class about the Constitution. I happily agreed.

Having never spoken to a class before, I figured that I had to fully prepare myself. I could think of no better way to communicate to school kids than to have a few giveaways. So, prior to going to the school, I visited the Jimmy Carter Library and Museum and purchased pencils with the preamble printed on them. I also bought a few Constitution booklets to give out.

After briefly sharing my background with the students, I discussed the Constitution and how it fits into their young lives. Afterward, the kids were full of questions. They all seemed to enjoy themselves. Ms. Hoskins was pleased with the lecture, too, and later invited me to come back to her class the next year. As for me, I felt great about being able to spark an interest in the little patriots of America.

After leaving Ms. Hoskins' class, I went to Taylor's second-grade class because she had told her teacher that I would be there. The teacher, Ms. Davis, invited me to speak to her class. It was truly wonderful seeing the second-graders learning about George Washington and the United States.

I have a few pocket-size Constitution booklets, and I keep one in my possession every day. I also have a few full-size Constitution books, but I cherish the pocket-size ones the most. I enjoy reading them and I am never without something to read.

My growing interest in the Constitution, politics, and history prompted me to try to see, hear, and even talk with dignitaries from politics, the military, and other important walks of life. Over the years, I have gotten autographs of some of these dignitaries in two of my Constitution booklets.

Senator Elizabeth Dole of North Carolina was the first. She was running for president in the 2000 Republican primaries. My co-worker Leslie White and I went to hear her speak at the Atlanta Fulton County Library on July 16, 1999. She chose the occasion to speak about kids getting access to porn via the Internet at libraries. Afterward, she was more than happy to honor my request for her autograph.

On November 11, 2003, I attended the Veterans Day Parade on Peachtree Street in Atlanta. Arriving a little early, I was able to meet the grand marshal, Governor Sonny Perdue. I asked him to sign my Constitution booklet, and he was honored to do so.

On June 17, 2004, I attended a book-signing reception. The book is titled *Medal of Honor, Portraits of Valor Beyond the Call of Duty*, by author Peter Collier and photographer Nick Del Calzo. The reception was at the National Museum of Patriotism in Atlanta. Jack H. Jacobs of the U.S. Army and Mi-

chael E. Thornton of the U.S. Navy, both Medal of Honor recipients, were in attendance. They both were gracious enough
to autograph my Constitution booklet.

On October 15, 2003, I attended a Racial Reconciliation
Forum hosted by Governor Perdue at the Jimmy Carter Library and Museum. While at the forum, I politely asked President Carter if he could autograph my Constitution booklet. He
said he could not because his wife was waiting for him, but
he promised to sign it if I would send it to him. I was disappointed that he declined to sign it, but there was no way that I
would put my Constitution booklet in the mail. Maybe I will
get another chance for him to sign it.

The United States is full of outstanding black patriots. On
November 11, 1999, Veterans Day, I got to meet such a pa-
triot: Jim Blaylock, who works at the Veterans Affairs Medical
Center in Decatur, Georgia, as the prosthetics chief.

Blaylock was interviewed by the *Atlanta Journal-Constitution* and gave the following account of his ordeal: In June
1967, Blaylock was a 21-year-old Marine Medivac helicopter
pilot. Blaylock's helicopter was shot down while attempting
to rescue thirteen Marines in Vietnam. Once his helicopter
landed, he was severely wounded by a rocket launcher, eventually losing a hand. He was presumed dead and was taken to
the morgue. Later, a mortician saw him bleeding and realized
he was still alive! The medics brought him back to conscious-
ness. In 1973, Blaylock began receiving treatment at the VA
hospital and eventually got a part-time job there. He has been
working there every since.

After reading his story, I decided I must meet this patriot.
In 1999, Blaylock served as the Veterans Day Parade grand
marshal in Atlanta. I had saved the newspaper that day, hoping
to get his autograph. I greeted Blaylock as the parade entrants
were being assembled. When I asked for his autograph, he was

surprised that I had kept the article and wanted his autograph. Meeting Blaylock was a moment that I will never forget.

*

I am constantly looking for opportunities to instill patriotism and love of our country in my children. One great vehicle for doing so was the Olympic Games, which came to Atlanta in August 1996. Also, the Games were a great opportunity to learn about other countries of the world. Reggie was 5 years old and Taylor was only 3. Nevertheless, they enjoyed the Games a great deal.

A week before the Games started, the kids and I headed to Centennial Olympic Park for its opening ceremony. We first located the Olympic brick with their names on it, a nice memento that we visit from time to time even today. Then the kids became some of the first to enjoy the Olympic Rings Water Fountain.

Congressman John Lewis was on hand for the ceremony. Reggie was happy to pose for a photo with him. Taylor, on the other hand, was a little afraid to get out of her stroller to sit with him.

During the Games, the kids and I toured the headquarters of numerous countries. They felt like they were traveling to a different country with each stop. The 1996 Olympic Games were spectacular, and we came away with great memories.

Of course, the most tragic moment of the Games happened when the bomb exploded in Centennial Olympic Park. The city was stunned by this terrorist act. The blast killed one person, Alice Hawthorne, and injured many more.

City and Olympic officials did not know whether the public would return to the park once it reopened. I guess everyone was surprised to see the turnout at the reopening. From my office on the 32nd floor of the 191 Peachtree Tower building,

I saw a sea of people on Andrew Young International Boulevard waiting to enter. At lunchtime, I joined the mourners in the park at the bomb site. The outpouring of love from the spectators—the flowers, teddy bears, signs, and other items left at the bomb site in memory of Alice Hawthorne—showed a compassionate and caring side of not just Atlantans, but citizens from around the world. May God be with Alice Hawthorne and her family.

By 1997, I was truly through with the Democratic Party. The Clinton administration and its minions and sycophants had totally turned me away from them. Still, I was able to maintain my respect for the presidency, if not the president himself. I wanted to pass along this respect for the presidency to my kids.

In early 1997, I visited the White House Web site and saw that it had a section for kids. There was even a page where kids could write to the president. Reggie and Taylor were already becoming computer savvy, so I called them to the computer. They got on the kids' section of the Web site and began clicking away. They learned about the White House pets, Socks the cat and Buddy the dog. They also learned about past presidents. I pointed out to them that President George H.W. Bush was in office when they were born, although it took a little explaining to help Taylor see that Bush, not President Clinton, was in office when she was born because her birthday was January 12, 1993. She barely snuck in under Bush's presidency.

After the kids wrote brief letters to Clinton and the White House pets, a surprise note came in the mail addressed to them. Clinton had sent a signed note, complete with the Presidential Seal, thanking Reggie and Taylor for writing to him. Even Socks, the "First Cat," sent a photo to them, complete with a paw print. We were all excited about this. We soon framed the presidential note and the photo of Socks, which today still hang in our dining room. Reggie and Taylor both know how much I support President Bush, and they understand that hanging these objects shows my respect for the presidency.

Another great way I have discovered to increase your love of your country is to travel around in it. As we know, there are many things to see, do, and learn in our country. My girlfriend, Peggy, really likes to travel, so I didn't have to do much to convince her to team up to hit the road with the kids and view the country.

In June 2000, we decided to drive from Atlanta to California with six kids, a first-grader through a sixth-grader. Overall, the trip was great. We had fun and learned quite a bit without turning the odyssey into a history class. Driving across Texas was a great indicator of the size of the country. Visiting places such as the Grand Canyon, Carlsbad Caverns, and the Living Desert showed the great contrasts of the country. Disneyland was probably the high point for the kids. Driving to Chavez Ravine and sitting in the stands of Dodger Stadium was one of my high points, even though the Men in Blue were off that day.

Our next great adventure was definitely a learning experience. In June 2001, we took another vacation trip. We titled our trip the "Black History and American History Tour." Our plan was to visit state capitol buildings of the states up the East coast, while stopping to visit black history sites as well.

Our first stop was Charleston, South Carolina. From there, we visited the capitol buildings of Raleigh, North Carolina; Richmond, Virginia; Washington, D.C.; Annapolis, Maryland; Harrisburg, Pennsylvania; and Trenton, New Jersey.

While visiting Richmond, it was nice to see Arthur Ashe's statue on Monument Avenue. I recalled the controversy about the placement of Ashe's statue on Monument Avenue amongst the Confederate generals.

Washington was memorable. It was good getting back to my old stomping grounds. We all enjoyed going to the Frederick Douglass Museum and House. The Jefferson Memorial was great, also.

Annapolis was pretty cool. My friend Gerard, his wife, Ginnie, and their son Malik gave us a guided tour of Gerard's hometown. We really had fun when we went swimming in the Chesapeake Bay. The Naval Academy was nice to see.

Down at the docks in town, we came across a statue of Alex Haley, the author of the book *Roots*. On the capitol grounds, there is a fine statue of former Supreme Court Justice Thurgood Marshall. Also on the capitol grounds is a statue of former Supreme Court Justice Roger Taney sitting in a big chair looking rather stately. I gave a quick history lesson to the kids, informing them that Taney was the chief justice during the Dred Scott trial.

Visiting Baltimore was quite moving. Besides going to the Inner Harbor and riding by Camden Yards, we could not pass up going to Fort McHenry, the site where Francis Scott Key wrote "The Star-Spangled Banner." While riding through Baltimore, we came across another statue of Justice Taney looking stately.

Next on our itinerary in Baltimore was The National Great Blacks in Wax Museum. The museum has on display life-like wax figures of famous blacks. Then we came across an exhibit of someone in a courtroom on trial. Lo and behold, it was Dred Scott, with Justice Taney standing over him yelling and pointing his finger at Scott!

I got excited and called the kids over. I said, "Now this is the Roger Taney I know." It was truly a time for a history lesson. Class was in session. I went more in depth about Dred Scott and the fact that he was a slave in Missouri. Over a twelve-year period, Scott traveled with his master, Dr. John Emerson, to Illinois and the Wisconsin Territory, where slavery was prohibited. Then they traveled back to Missouri. After Dr. Emerson died, his wife, Irene, became Scott's master.

Scott and his wife Harriet sued Mrs. Emerson for their freedom. Scott said, "Once free, always free," considering that he had traveled to free territories. The case eventually went to the U.S. Supreme Court. Chief Justice Taney and some of the other justices disagreed with Scott. This decision basically helped fuel the Civil War.

While I was telling the kids the story of Dred Scott, a reporter and camera crew from television station WBAL in Baltimore listened intently. They enjoyed the lesson so much that they asked me to repeat it so they could film it for their evening newscast. Of course I obliged. I was more than happy to tell the other side of Justice Taney, who was looking quite stately elsewhere in Maryland.

Touring Philadelphia was truly an American adventure. The Liberty Bell and the African-American Museum, complete with a sculpture honoring Crispus Attucks, were enjoyable. The kids especially liked touring the Philadelphia Mint and seeing money being coined.

My favorite part of the trip was touring Independence Hall and seeing the chair that George Washington used during the Constitutional Convention in 1787. The Rising Sun Chair, or a replica of it, conjured up thoughts of the debates that went on about the Constitution. Being in Independence Hall was the icing on the cake of a great Black History and American History Tour.

I must say that visiting Trenton, New Jersey, was strange. First of all, there is a sign that says "Trenton makes, the world takes." That did not make much sense to us. Then we couldn't find the highway exit for the capitol. It was as if the state did not want visitors at the capitol. We even pulled over and asked for directions to the capitol, to no avail. One person did not even know that the capitol was in Trenton! There was another lesson for the kids—know your state capitol.

*

Sometimes history comes to you. One such event happened in April 2002, when the Jimmy Carter Library and Museum hosted a traveling exhibit called The Declaration of Independence Road Trip, with the main attraction being one of the original Dunlap Broadsides of the Declaration of Independence. With my great interest in American history, I had to see this.

Opening day of the exhibit, April 27, was a great day to visit the Carter Library. I dressed up in my signature American flag necktie for the occasion. Seeing the Dunlap Broadside was thrilling. I took a few pictures and collected some souvenirs.

Outside the Carter Library, a somewhat delightful occurrence happened. A group of women from the Daughters of the American Revolution was milling about outside. They were all dressed up, some in red, white, and blue. Some had ribbons and sashes representing their organization. I knew a little about their group's history, particularly its past views on blacks. Nevertheless, they were there for the same reason I was.

When they saw me, several of them complimented me on my American flag necktie. I thanked them and truly appreciated their compliments. We talked briefly about the Dunlap Broadside. Later, I asked if I could take a picture with one of them. The nice lady obliged and someone took the photo with my camera. Later in the day, I told someone about my experience and she said, "Do you know about their history?" I said, "Yeah, but at the time I thought about Rodney King and his famous words: 'Can't we all just get along?'"

*

I had another encounter with history on March 15, 2003, a cloudy and dreary day, when radio station WGST sponsored a Rally for America at Centennial Olympic Park. The rally was held to rally our citizens as well as to show support for our troops who were beginning the war in Iraq. WGST Radio host Kim Peterson was there, along with nationally syndicated radio talk show host Glenn Beck. One of the special guests was Medal of Honor recipient General Raymond G. Davis. The crowd was estimated at 25,000 to 30,000.

As the peaceful crowd grew larger and larger, we wondered why there were no news media personnel to witness and televise this outpouring of support for our troops. CNN's absence was particularly glaring, considering that Centennial Olympic Park is located across the street from its world headquarters. The CNN powers-that-be merely needed to look out their windows to view the sea of patriots. Maybe they were on the other side of town, covering the pro-Saddam get-together. Hours later, CNN did send a camera crew to cover the event.

General Davis came to the stage to thunderous applause. He stated that he was pleased to see all the people who had come out to show support for our troops. I had heard of Davis and his many accomplishments, and I was glad to finally see and hear him speak. The general, a Georgia Tech graduate, had served his country in the United States Marine Corps and reached the rank of commandant of the Marines. He had joined the National Museum of Patriotism as a board member. The museum has a beautiful display of him, complete with his Medal of Honor.

General Davis passed away on September 3, 2003. He was a true patriot, and his untiring efforts for the cause of freedom will be missed.

*

After hearing so much about Georgia Senator Zell Miller's book, *A National Party No More: The Conscience of a Conservative Democrat*, I figured that I had to go buy it. I had read excerpts in the newspapers and on the Internet, and had seen and heard him interviewed on television and on the radio, so by the time I purchased the book, I felt that I had practically read it and knew all its content already. Nevertheless, I knew I must add his book to my library.

Miller scheduled a few book signings in the area, so on November 28, 2003, I felt it was a must to go get my copy of his book autographed. He had written in his book about being punctual, so I knew that I had to get to the book signing early. Miller was scheduled to begin autographing at 10 a.m., so I arrived at approximately 9:15 a.m. However, he had already begun signing books.

Meeting Senator Miller was great! Naturally, I had to wear my signature American flag necktie for the special occasion; it is not often you meet your senator. He even complimented me, saying, "Hey, I like that tie." When I posed to get my picture taken, he said, "Make sure you get a picture of that tie."

After he signed my book, I said to him, "Sir I would be honored if you could sign my Constitution." He did it with no questions asked. He told me, "Glad to see you are carrying it around."

I highly recommend Miller's book. The most amazing thing in it is how he talked about his mom, Birdie Bryan Miller, wading in cold mountain water, selecting rock after rock, and piling them on the creek bank, later to be taken to a field where she and others built their house. Miller was an infant at that time. To this day, he and his wife, Shirley, live in that house.

I brought my two kids' Constitution booklets along also in hopes of getting those autographed by Miller. I did not want to hold up the line, so I waited until the line died down later. When I went back into the bookstore, I asked Miller if he could sign my kids' Constitution booklets, and he graciously obliged.

While standing in line, one older lady asked him if he was going to be there for a little while. She said she wanted to purchase some books for his autograph. Later, while I was sitting down reading Jesse Lee Peterson's book, *Scam*, I saw the lady again. I asked her if she had gotten her books signed. She said yes and said that she had bought four books, which entitled her to get a book free. Then she asked me if I was Miller's driver. I chuckled and said no. Then she asked me if I was with him. Again I said no and calmly explained that I had come to get my book autographed, too.

Being that she was white, I could have taken offense and said something like, "What do you think this is, *Driving Miss Daisy?*" But the fact that she did not realize I was there for the same reason she was did not upset me. After all, why should I choose to get upset over someone's ignorance? Of course, I know some people would have been nonplussed. Actually, in my earlier years, I would have been upset about this. But now I figure life is too short to let things of this nature affect my day negatively.

*

Learning about the Constitution led me to take more of an interest in American history, a subject that I found quite boring while in school. Surprisingly though, as I began to do my own research on American history and formulating a historical timeline of events in American and world history, things that I had learned in school started to come back to me and fall in place. Plus, studying American history allowed me to integrate black history and American history rather than treating them as individual subjects, for black history *is* American history.

Through practically every historical event in America, blacks have been there. Every war that America was involved in—from the Revolutionary War, in which Crispus Attucks was the first casualty, to the Buffalo Soldiers, to World War II with the Tuskegee Airmen—blacks were there. We have all seen the painting of the crossing of the Delaware, with George Washington and his crew crossing over to New Jersey to surprise the drunken Hessians. But have you taken a close look at his crew and spotted the black man, Prince Whipple, rowing. Look closely, near Washington's right knee. Or what about Jocko Graves, whom Washington sent ahead of him and his crew to gather horses across the river? He was found frozen, but still holding onto the horses' reins. Ever heard of a man named York? You will have to dig a little to find out about this black slave who was a member of the Lewis and Clark expedition party.

Whenever I see the portrait "The Surrender of Cornwallis" by John Trumbull, the artist of the Revolution, I am reminded of one of my favorite people of the Revolutionary War, James Armistead. Armistead was a slave but, during the war, he became a spy, a double agent, in fact. He spied on Benedict Arnold and reported back to the Marquis de Lafayette. The information he passed along to Lafayette was quite instrumental in the defeat of Lord Cornwallis at Yorktown, Virginia, on October 19, 1781.

A couple of days after Cornwallis surrendered, he went to the headquarters of Lafayette. While discussing the war, Cornwallis looked up and saw Armistead. Only then did he realize that he had been set up by Armistead. For his loyalty, Armistead was given his freedom.

Armistead's story is just one of many about blacks who played integral roles in our country's wars and history. Blacks have contributed to the growth and prosperity of this country, with much of the contribution coming in the form of free labor. Blacks have fought and died for this country. If you build something, even if you are forced to build it, you feel more of a part of it than if it was given to you. With this in mind, I believe that I and other blacks should feel much more American than any other race of people here, save for the American Indians. After all, our black ancestors helped build the United States, so what better way to pay homage to them than to claim and pledge allegiance to this country? Being black and looking at all the sacrifices my ancestors made makes me feel obligated to honor their struggle. By being a patriot of this country, I am paying homage to my forefathers.

*

How about Democrats? Can they be patriotic? Absolutely! A person's party affiliation does not preclude anyone from being a patriot. Whether a person is a Democrat, Republican, or independent, he or she can show love for the good old U.S. of A.

But what if a person supports one party and the president of the United States is of another party? Should that person's patriotism wane? Of course not! A true patriot does not turn patriotism—the love of one's country—on and off based on what party is in the White House. Shamefully, though, it happens.

One case in point regards the state of Georgia's license plate. Georgia has several license plate designs from which to choose. One is a wildlife license plate with a bald eagle, an American flag, and the phrase "Give Wildlife a Chance." According to an *Atlanta Journal-Constitution* article dated February 17, 2004, "Money from sales of the license plates—$19 of the $20 annual fee—goes to the Georgia Wildlife Resources Division, which uses the funds to buy wilderness areas and pay biologists to study the state's plants and animals." If you are an environmentalist, you probably would think that this program is a good thing. But not so fast!

The *Atlanta Journal-Constitution* article stated that one environmentalist "dislikes what he sees as a red-white-and blue symbol of political views he doesn't share." The environmentalist was quoted as saying: "Why did [the state] pick that tag? I have friends who refuse to buy it because it's so rah-rah. . . . I'm a patriot, but I'm not a gun-toting, flag-waving, Bush-loving patriot."

The article went on to state that "the new plate poses a dilemma for some environmentalists. . . . In Georgia, as elsewhere, many of them lean to Democratic or Green Party candidates. Some see a connection between flag-waving symbols and President Bush, who they say favors big business over the environment. When pushed, many say they don't support the U.S. war effort in Iraq."

This is exactly what I mean. If the environmentalists were truly patriots, it would not matter who is in the Oval Office. Besides, Republicans do not hold ownership to our American flag, bald eagle, or any of the other patriotic symbols of America that we hold so dear. Sadly, this is the state of patriotism in some corners of America.

Even Jerry McCollum, chief executive officer of the Georgia Wildlife Federation, said he did not like the tag when it was introduced. He is quoted in the article as saying, "I thought it was feeding off the patriotic mood our country was in." And what is wrong with that?

Frankly, I feel that we need even more things such as Georgia's patriotic—I mean, wildlife—license plate to foster patriotism. When it came time for me to renew my license plate, you can be sure that I got mine. And I definitely was not alone. The *Atlanta Journal-Constitution*'s article stated that in the first two months of sales, the license plate brought in $946,941, more than half what the old tag averaged over an entire year! Hurray for Georgia's patriots!

*

On November 28, 2001, Atlanta's then-Mayor Bill Campbell gave a welcome statement to the State of the Black World Conference in Atlanta. Among other things, he said, "While the rest of the country waves the flag of Americana, we understand we are not part of that." Excuse me? Campbell needs to speak for himself.

The day after Campbell made that ridiculous statement, my place of employment had a send-off for a colleague who had been called up by the U.S. Army Reserve. He was going off to war. As our colleague stated, "We feel like family." The blacks, whites, and Muslims of our company presented him cards, gifts, poems, jokes, handshakes, and hugs as if we were sending off our own blood brother.

That man, along with countless other black men and women of this country, is putting his life on the line to protect our country, and yet Campbell and the like carry so much hatred for their country that they cannot understand or appreciate these black servicemen and women, as well as the others serving our country. Neither can he appreciate the America that got him elected to office.

Of course, we know he was not speaking for all black people, but his comments were still a shame because, since he was the mayor at the time, he had some influence over some of the kids of this city. Hopefully one day Campbell will learn about and appreciate the black forefathers who have fought for this country since the Revolutionary War. Maybe one day he will discover this country's black citizens, who are among the most patriotic and who are ensconced in Americana—baseball and apple pie, included.

*

Then there is Mom. One summer weekend in 2003, I visited my mom in North Carolina. Mom has had an American flag flying from a tree in the front yard for quite a while. But on this visit, the flag was upside down! "Mom, why do you have the flag upside down?" I asked. In reply, she went into her "I-can't-stand-Bush" diatribe.

I then told her, "President Bush does not have anything to do with the flag. He is just the president. "Don't you love this country?"

"Sure," she said. "I support our troops, too. I just don't like Bush."

Later in the day, I went to the tree, grabbed the flag down, and placed it right-side up. I put it up higher, where she could not reach it. Of course, she got on me about messing with her flag.

"Boy, put my flag back like I had it!" she said.

"No, Mom," I said. "If you don't like President Bush, show it some other way, but not with the flag."

When she went out to the tree and saw that she could not reach the flag, I started laughing. She could not reach Old Glory, so she had to leave it right-side up.

Later that summer, in August, my birthday rolled around. Mom sent me a birthday card. After reading the lovely card, I noticed an American flag stamp on the envelope. You guessed it—it was upside down! I immediately picked up the phone and called her. She started laughing. I guess she got the last laugh.

6

Coming out of the
Republican Closet

———

Even with all the facts and rumors that were coming out about then-Governor Bill Clinton, I still supported him during his first presidential campaign. By this time, I was a faithful listener of Rush Limbaugh and Neal Boortz. Both Limbaugh and Boortz preached about Clinton's character flaws. But I still voted for candidate Clinton. I voted with my race rather than my brain.

On the night Clinton was elected, I felt great! I had participated in our political process by voting. Thoughts of my ancestors fighting and dying to vote weighed on my mind. I thought about how, in the past, tests had been given to some blacks to see if they qualified to vote. They were asked questions such as "How many bubbles are there in a bar of soap?"

Somehow, everyone failed the test. By voting, particularly for Clinton, a Democrat, I felt I had done my ancestors proud.

That was in November 1992. By the summer of 1993, I had begun to question my vote for Clinton.

Clinton's first term had started off rather shakily. It was a year of uncertainty, disappointment, and a big "I told you so" from Limbaugh regarding character. There was the "Don't ask, don't tell" policy about gays in the military. Then there was "Travelgate," in which long-time White House employees were fired so the Clintons could hire their own staff. Putting their own people on staff was not necessarily bad, but the Clintons went about it in a harsh way. They put the FBI onto Travel Office Director Billy Dale and other staff members. Criminal charges were brought up against Dale and his staff, and they were fired, only later to be exonerated.

The real kicker for me was "Filegate." Hundreds of FBI personnel files on the Clintons' political friends and foes were obtained by the White House from the FBI. Clinton called it an "honest bureaucratic snafu." But can you imagine having damaging personal information on your political enemies as well as your friends? Over the years, I came to feel that Clinton got away with so much because he had the FBI files on his detractors.

By the time of the 1994 congressional elections, I was beginning to get disgruntled with the Democratic Party. Congressman Newt Gingrich represented my district, but I don't think I ever had the courage to vote for him before he moved to another district. His "Contract with America" sounded quite appealing, though. I was for the "Contract," but I was not yet swayed to vote for a Republican.

*

The National Association for the Advancement of Colored

People held a forum on welfare reform on January 10, 1996. At the time, talk show host Sean Hannity was working with radio station WGST. I was a big fan of his show. I guess I was "Hannitized" before "Hannitization" was invented. Hannity was invited to join Congressman John Lewis and a few others on the panel. The public was invited also, so I decided to attend. I thought the forum might be worth attending because it was as if Hannity was going into the lion's den.

The forum was held at the Auburn Avenue Library, a few blocks from my office in downtown Atlanta. I arrived early in order to get a seat up front in the auditorium. After a few greetings, the organizers asked a minister on the panel to open the forum with a prayer—a great way to start, you might think. But while the minister was praying, he started chastising Republicans. Talk about blasphemy! Never had I heard of someone praying like this! Even Hannity spoke up afterward about how wrong it was to say a prayer like that. The discussion went downhill from there.

Hannity was the only conservative on the panel. The others tried to bombard him with liberal thoughts and questions. Of course, Hannity stood his ground. I had his back to a degree. Lewis spoke up about subsidies, and I chimed in with "Yeah, peanut subsidies!" Peanut farming was heavily subsidized in Georgia at the time, and Lewis was a peanut subsidy supporter. Lewis glared at me.

Later on, the discussion turned to the NAACP. I stood up and asked why the NAACP caters only to Democrats and does not support blacks who are conservative or Republican. A female of the NAACP stood up to say that the NAACP does have Republican members. At that, Hannity asked about joining the NAACP. He pulled out his cash and joined the NAACP on the spot. When the panel discussion was over, I went up to the stage, shook hands with Hannity, and congratulated him on a job well done.

When I left the building, an older gentleman who was in the audience told me that I was wrong for trying to support Republicans. He said something to the effect that I did not understand what blacks had gone through. I told him that I did understand and we needed blacks to be supportive of both parties.

In January 1996, my place of employment had not yet designated Martin Luther King Jr. Day as a holiday. Considering that our office is located in Atlanta, the birthplace of Dr. King, I thought seriously about asking my company's office president to go to the ceremony at Ebenezer Baptist Church with me. Instead, I just went to view the MLK Day March down Peachtree Street. Later, after watching the news of the event at Ebenezer Baptist Church, I thanked God I had not asked him to go.

During that time of the year, first lady Hillary Clinton was in hot water over the Whitewater files and the Rose law firm's missing billing records. Also, just two months before that, Gingrich had to exit through the rear door of Air Force One, a show of disrespect on President Clinton's behalf, after returning from Israeli Premier Yitzhak Rabin's funeral with Clinton and others.

During the MLK Day ceremony at Ebenezer Baptist Church, one speaker began criticizing Gingrich for complaining about going out the rear door of Air Force One. The speaker said something to the effect that, "Now Gingrich knows how blacks feel." Then there were comments about Republicans trying to go after Hillary Clinton regarding the Whitewater files and the Rose firm's billing records. "Hold on Hillary, hold on" was shouted from the pulpit. It was as if the King Holiday had been turned into a "Bash Republicans Day," and in the sanctuary of Ebenezer Baptist Church, no less! What have we blacks come to? Using the church to demonize political foes! I was very glad I had not asked my company office president to attend that hate fest.

During the 1996 presidential campaign, I felt compelled to vote for Senator Bob Dole, even though I knew he would not win. I made up my mind that I was going to vote my conscience and vote with my brain, using the knowledge that I had gained through all my research. I felt it was high time to vote the way I knew I should and not vote for a party just because the majority of blacks would vote for that party or would vote for Clinton because he seemed likely to win.

Even after voting for Dole, I told very few people that I had done so. What I did get up the nerve to say most of the time, without revealing who I had voted for, was that I felt blacks should not have all their eggs in one basket. I guess I used this as my personal excuse for voting Republican.

In 1998, the Monica Lewinsky scandal was dominating the news. Clinton testified before a grand jury on August 17, 1998. With my constitutional beliefs, the fact that he lied under oath truly dismayed me.

For a number of years, I had been schooled by talk radio, columnists, the Internet, Fox News, and other sources that provided viewpoints other than that of the mainstream media, which is Democratic-leaning. I had been influenced through all my listening to talk radio; by being "Hannitized" by Sean Hannity; by being a student of the "Limbaugh Institute for Advanced Conservative Studies," run by Rush Limbaugh; and by being a congregation member of the "Church of the Painful Truth" under "High Priest" Neal Boortz. I had read books and columns by Walter E. Williams, Thomas Sowell, Larry Elder, Star Parker, Ken Hamlin, Armstrong Williams, and John McWhorter, all of whom are black Americans who are highly respected in their professions. Ann Coulter was a favorite of mine, also. In addition, I had researched the Constitution and other historical documents to get a better understanding of the roots of our government and what exactly government's role in our lives should be. After exposing myself to all this information and gaining knowledge, I came to the conclusion that I am politically conservative. But I did not say this out loud. I kept it to myself.

During the 1998 Christmas holidays, Mom came from North Carolina to visit us. She stayed at the home of my brother Michael. I had previously discussed with my family my displeasure with Clinton and the Democratic Party, but only to a certain degree. This would truly be a Christmas to remember.

While at Michael's house, Mom and I began discussing Clinton and his peccadilloes, specifically Monica Lewinsky. Soon, our conversation went from a discussion to a heated debate to a shouting match! I was trying to have a discussion on the topic of Democrats and Republicans, but I could not get a word in edgewise. Mom simply refused to hear me out. Every time I would try to explain my position, she would shout me down.

As Michael recorded the "discussion" with his camcorder, I tried to talk about the fact that, according to the Constitution, the president should "protect and defend the Constitution" and not send his subordinates to lie to one of the branches that the Constitution established, the judiciary. In between me trying to get that statement out and Mom badgering me by saying "It was just sex," I spontaneously began to recite the preamble to the Constitution. "We the People of the United States. . . ." It was the only thing I could say or do.

Well, I did say one other thing. I shouted out, "By the way, I voted for Bob Dole!" Then I began to let it all out. "Yeah, I am a Republican—and proud of it!" I said. "I am sick and tired of the Democratic Party using black people. We have been voting for Democrats for the longest time. Every time Clinton gets in trouble, he runs to us blacks to bail him out. He goes to the black church with the biggest Bible you ever seen!"

I got quite a few political issues off my chest that night. Once I did, I felt relieved. The weight of my race on my back to remain a Democrat was lifted. I decided right then and there that I would freely speak my mind about my conservative and Republican beliefs. I realized that I was coming out of the Republican closet!

You would have thought I had admitted that I was gay! Like so many Democrats, rather than debating and having a conversation, Mom continued to shout me down because of my conservative beliefs.

*

On October 30, 2002, I attended a rally for Saxby Chambliss, who was running for the U.S. Senate against incumbent Max Cleland. Chambliss could not attend the event because, as we were told by his fill-in, Congressman Mac Collins, Chambliss was in Washington, D.C., filming commercials. While at the rally, I inquired about getting tickets for President Bush's upcoming visit. I was told to visit Chambliss' office in Atlanta to get some tickets. I couldn't think of a better way to show that I was out of the Republican closet than by going to see the head Republican.

The next morning, I called to reserve four tickets. On my lunch hour, I went to pick them up. I was really excited to have tickets to see Bush. I got extra tickets in case I could find someone else who wanted to go, but no such luck.

That Saturday, November 2, I headed out to the Cobb Galleria Centre in my signature American flag necktie. I knew I had to arrive early to get a good viewing spot. I arrived around 7 a.m., waiting for the doors to open at 8. After being let inside the lobby, we had to wait in line another thirty minutes or so before being let into the hall. Once we got in the hall, we were given American flags and red, white, and blue pom-poms.

Being that I was in the initial group that entered the hall, I was able to get up front in the standing area near the stage. That was the good news. The bad news was that we were told at the rally that the president would not arrive until around noon! Standing around was tiring. Fortunately, I had brought my Spanish homework and flash cards to pass the time. Plus, the surrounding group of people got to know one another. We exchanged e-mail addresses with one gentleman who had a digital camera so he could send us some photos.

As time passed, more and more people began to fill in the standing-room area. We long-time standers had to keep our position at the front. Eventually, the Presidential Seal was brought out and mounted on the lectern. That really got the crowd going. Then the Secret Service came by to collect the pom-poms and flags from those of us who were up front. They wanted to avoid someone accidentally sticking Bush just in case he came our way to greet us. Lucky for me, I had a shoulder bag and placed mine in it before they were confiscated. They also said there would be no autographs.

Soon the local politicians came out to say a few words. Senatorial candidate Saxby Chambliss and congressional candidate Phil Gingrey spoke, along with Governor Sonny Perdue and a few others.

Finally, Bush came out! The crowd went wild! Waiting all that time had paid off. Seeing the president in person brought back memories of working with Air Force One and seeing President Reagan and President Bush's dad all the time.

Bush gave an uplifting speech to the audience. He talked about the fine Republican candidates from Georgia. I was so excited, I called my sister, Lillian, and told her I was at a President Bush rally. Being that she is conservative, she was excited to know I was at the rally.

After his speech, Bush headed toward the steps, shaking hands as he went. As he came by our area, I reached out and shook his hand! That really made the wait worthwhile. I attempted to get him to sign my Constitution booklet, but he was moving too fast. I was able to take a photo of him as he was shaking the hands of the others in my group. We all were ecstatic about shaking Bush's hand.

Afterward, I left the Cobb Galleria Centre pumped up. I called Mom with my exciting news. I had told her earlier in the week that I was going to the rally, so she knew I was there. I said, "Mom, I saw President Bush and he shook my hand!" Mom deadpanned, "Well, has your hand fell off yet?" I could only laugh.

Later the next week, the gentleman to whom we had given our e-mail addresses sent us some photos he had taken. He also sent the address of the White House Web site, where the White House staff had posted some photos from the rally. While looking at the photos, I noticed my hand in the air waving. I called Taylor and Reggie in to see my hand on the White House Web site. Then Taylor said, "Daddy there you are in the picture." Lo and behold, my face was peering out from the surrounding people. I copied the photo and blew it up to verify it was me. Sure enough, I had made it to the White House Web site! What a way to cap off a great weekend.

*

On April 3, 2003, former Congressman J.C. Watts, Jr. came to town to promote his book, *What Color Is a Conservative? My Life and My Politics.* He went on Boortz's radio show to discuss issues and his book, and he mentioned that he was having a book signing at a local bookstore. I was eager to meet Watts because I admired him for being the lone black conservative in Congress, so I decided to go to the book signing. I actually spoke with him briefly while he signed my book.

Reading Watts' book and speaking with him helped inspire

me to write my own book. Our stories have some similarities in that when you are black and conservative, arrows get fired your way from fellow blacks who do not want other blacks to think for themselves.

*

There was a time in my life when I would not have freely admitted that I wanted to visit the Ronald Reagan Library & Museum, but I had wanted to go there for some time to pay homage to my former commander-in-chief. I got to go just recently.

In May 2004, Peggy and I made reservations to vacation in Los Angeles. She had lived there and still had family and friends in the area, so she would be the perfect tour guide for me. The Reagan Library was number one on my itinerary. We scheduled vacation dates from July 15 through 19, with plans to visit the museum on Saturday, July 17.

On June 5, 2004, while we were in Canada, we got the sad news that Reagan had died. I soon began reflecting on my time working with Air Force One.

The outpouring of admiration worldwide for Reagan was gratifying to see. At Niagara Falls, the United States flags were flown at half-staff to show respect for him. The media's reflection of Reagan was a pleasant surprise, as well. Some in the media got in jabs on Reagan, but overall the coverage was great.

Reagan always had his admirers, but I think that, over time, more and more people came to appreciate what he accomplished by ending the Cold War. I especially liked how Reagan had brought patriotism back into vogue during his presidency.

When we got to Los Angeles, we decided to visit the museum on Thursday, July 15, rather than on Saturday, hoping that the crowd would not be as large. Driving up to the museum was quite moving. Banners of all the former presidents hang from light poles lining the street. At the entrance of the museum, we saw flowers and mementos from Reagan's funeral still displayed. The tour of the museum also was quite fascinating, with all the memorabilia.

During the time of our visit, there was a traveling exhibit of Lewis and Clark artifacts on display. I was pleased to see a statue of York in the exhibit. The museum was not something Peggy would have put on her itinerary, but she was at least happy to see York on display.

Outside of the museum, there is a section of the Berlin Wall on display—a nice tribute to the man who was so instrumental in the wall being torn down. Also outside the museum is Reagan's burial site, which is touching. His is a fine final resting place, overlooking California.

Having visited the Reagan and Carter presidential libraries, I highly recommend both, although I find the Reagan Library more meaningful. Plus, I find it majestic, particularly the view.

Nowadays, I do not freely admit that I visit the Jimmy Carter Library on occasion without explaining my love of American history. Plus, I do not allow Carter to diminish my respect for the presidency, even though, in recent years, Carter has attempted to rebuild his battered image by tearing down others, particularly President Bush.

*

While in California, I got to do something else that I would have been too embarrassed to admit before. I attended a Bush-Cheney Party!

The Bush-Cheney campaign had scheduled Bush-Cheney Parties, complete with a conference call with first lady Laura

Bush, across the country on July 15, 2004. I had hoped to attend a party in the Atlanta area, but Peggy and I had already made plans to be at the Reagan Library in California on that day. So I went to the Bush Web site to see if I could locate a party near where I would be staying in the Los Angeles area. I discovered that Michael and Patricia Korpal, a fine Republican couple, were going to have a party in Pasadena. I corresponded to let them know that I would be coming from Atlanta.

Peggy and her friend, Linda, drove me to Pasadena for the party. Being that they are Democrats, Peggy and Linda said that they would drop me off and go to see the movie *Fahrenheit 9/11*. Very funny, I thought.

As we pulled up to the Korpals' house, we realized we were early. Thinking that I would be one of just a few black Republicans at the party, I jokingly said, "I hope they don't think I am the cook or waiter coming to serve everyone."

Michael greeted me at the door and was elated to see me. He said I was the first to RSVP for their party. He introduced me to Patricia, who also was elated to see me. She introduced me to the other guests and told them I had come all the way from Atlanta. Being that I had traveled the farthest, she said, "You are the star of the party!"

About twenty-five people attended the Korpals' party. After greeting one another, we ate and drank adult beverages while we waited for Mrs. Bush to call. We discussed President Bush's chances of being re-elected and other political issues. The Korpals passed out bumper stickers and other campaign material. I made myself the unofficial photographer for the party.

Mrs. Bush called around 5:30 p.m. Some of us stood in the kitchen and dining room while others sat in the den, listening intently to Mrs. Bush. She gave an uplifting pep talk and stressed the importance of what we were doing insofar as getting out the vote.

Before she ended the call, she said someone wanted to say a few words to us. Surprisingly, President Bush got on the telephone. Everyone was ecstatic to hear him. He thanked us for our support and urged us to keep up the work and continue to recruit others to the cause.

After the call, we all gathered in the den and talked about what had brought us to the cause. We all felt that Bush would be re-elected, but the Californians at the party were not optimistic about their state delivering its fifty-five electoral votes to the president.

After hearing the negatives about their state's chances, I had to chime in.

"Try to remain positive and keep plugging away at what you are doing," I said. "Look at my state of Georgia, for example. Georgia had been a Democratic state for the longest time. Now we are considered a Republican state and we even have Democratic Senator Zell Miller on our side. So take heart and keep doing what you are doing."

*

One disturbing site in California was the Arlington West Memorial Project at Santa Monica Beach. Crosses are placed in the sand, one for each soldier who has died in the war against terror in Iraq. I find it disturbing because I think the dead soldiers are being used as a political tool by the people who are against Bush and the war. Arlington West is a thoughtful project, but the motives are wrong. I was going to ask the project representatives why there are no crosses to represent the thousands who died in the terror attacks on September 11, 2001, but I decided to leave it alone. I also was going to tell them that I had been to the real Arlington Cemetery and that the soldiers there were not being used as political pawns like at Arlington West. But I figured, why bother?

7

Blacks and the Democratic Party: Their History and Relationship

Since John F. Kennedy reluctantly started supporting Dr. Martin Luther King Jr. and the civil-rights movement, blacks have had a strong and supportive relationship with the Democratic Party. After much review, I would like to evaluate this relationship.

Who was the first black president? Technically, no black has served as president yet. But that hasn't stopped some people from designating the first black president.

For example, black activist Dick Gregory claimed that John Hanson was black. Hanson was elected president by the Continental Congress in 1781 under the Articles of Confederation, which called for a president to serve a one-year term. Some people say the Articles of Confederation called for a president of the Congress, not of the United States. Six other presidents followed Hanson before the approval of the current Constitution. So John Hanson was president, either of the Continental Congress or of the United States, a nice trivia question. However, he certainly was not black.

Still, Gregory claimed on his Web site that Hanson was on the $2 bill in the Declaration of Independence portrait on the back of the note. But the Declaration of Independence portrait was of the signing of the document in 1776, a few years before the Articles of Confederation's adoption on March 1, 1781. In the portrait, John Hancock, the president of the Continental Congress, is at the head table. Gregory even has what looks to be a photo of Hanson on his Web site, even though cameras were not used at the time. I e-mailed Gregory with this information, but I did not receive a response. I wonder why?

Then there was President Clinton, whom author Toni Morrison called the first black president. She stated that because he was from a single-parent household, was born poor, was working-class, played the saxophone, and loved McDonald's and junk food, he was essentially a black man.

In March 2002, Senator John Kerry wanted to get in on the act. In an interview with the American Urban Radio Network, Kerry said, "President Clinton was often known as the first black president. I wouldn't be upset if I could earn the right to be the second." Are you kidding me! The gall! I was no supporter of Al Sharpton or Carol Moseley Braun, but was Kerry's comment not a slap in the face of these two blacks who were actually trying to become the first black president?

I truly think that Democrats began calling Clinton the first black president because some people wanted black people to not know how Frederick Douglass and others felt about President Lincoln, who was a Republican. "Know your history" is said throughout the black community, but this historical fact—that Lincoln was a Republican—is one some choose to forget or ignore.

The gathering, including Frederick Douglass, at Boston's Tremont Temple went wild celebrating the issuance of the Emancipation Proclamation on December 31, 1862. They knew more work was ahead of them to free all slaves, but they also knew that the Emancipation Proclamation was a new beginning. In response, Douglass called Lincoln the "black man's president."

I can hear some readers saying: "Lincoln did not free the slaves. The Emancipation Proclamation applied to the slaves in the Southern states, and being that those states were at war with the North, they were not about to abide by anything President Lincoln said." However, there is ample evidence of Lincoln's sincere desire to free the slaves.

In 1858, Lincoln was nominated to run against incumbent Senator Stephen A. Douglas. In his acceptance speech, Lincoln said: "A house divided against itself cannot stand. I believe this government cannot endure, permanently half slave and half free. I do not expect the Union to be dissolved—I do not expect the house to fall—but I do expect it will cease to be divided. It will become all one thing, or all the other. Either the opponents of slavery will arrest the further spread of it, and place it where the public mind shall rest in the belief that it is in the course of ultimate extension; or its advocates will push it forward till it shall become alike lawful in all the States—old as well as new, North as well as South."

Ever hear of the Crittenden Compromise? In 1860, Senator John Crittenden of Kentucky submitted a proposal to keep Southern states from leaving the Union. The compromise proposed amendments to the Constitution, basically in support of slavery. The compromise was defeated in part by President-elect Lincoln's opposition to it.

Then there is the letter Lincoln wrote on August 22, 1862, to Horace Greeley, editor of the *New York Tribune* newspaper. When the letter is read in its entirety, it provides a more complete understanding about Lincoln's feelings on saving the Union.

If you are still not convinced about Lincoln's sincerity, peruse the Gettysburg Address and see what message you can derive from it. Also read Lincoln's Inaugural Address of March 4, 1865. You might see him in a different light; God's beam of light upon him.

*

Rather than praise the rich people who have worked hard to become rich, Democrats lump all rich people together and denigrate them. They talk as if someone who is rich must be a bad person. Sure, they might single out a rich person here or there for praise, but it's rare. Sadly, some of the rich people they put down are in fact Democrats. Some, if you can believe it, are black. They will praise Robert Johnson, the founder of Black Entertainment Television, or they will honor Magic Johnson for his involvement in the community, but they also stereotype them as being rich and then begin to put them down.

Sure, there are some rich people who inherited their money. And that's okay. Let us not hate them. Is not that the level blacks are trying to obtain? Don't we want to be able to pass on an inheritance to our children? Besides, the more people who receive an inheritance, the less who need to rely on government and others for assistance. Or is that what some people really want—more people relying on the government?

*

When President Clinton, Mrs. Clinton, and the rest of his administration were getting in trouble by breaking the law or skirting the law, Democrats blindly supported them and even made excuses to cover up for them. They expressed agreement with so many things the Clinton administration did that they showed they had been led astray from the party's principles. Looking back, if the Democrats had admonished their own for their missteps, things would not have gotten out of hand with Clinton and the others. But because Democratic Party members made excuses and explained away so many wrong-doings, the Clinton administration got bolder as time went on. They knew their party would cover for them, and so would the mainstream media.

But take President Bush, on the other hand. Republican Party members have found numerous things about which to disagree with Bush. Plus, they have let their feelings about some of these disagreements be known.

*

Attorney Leo Terrell is a staunch Democrat and is a supporter of the National Association for the Advancement of Colored People (NAACP). At least he was, until the NAACP crossed him.

In June 2001, President Bush nominated Judge Carol Kuhl, a white female, to the 9th U.S. Circuit Court of Appeals. Having been before her in previous cases, Terrell knew Judge Kuhl and thought she would be an asset to the 9th Circuit Court. There were only a couple of problems. First, Bush, a Republican, had nominated her. Plus, from some accounts, she is pro-life. As we all know, the NAACP is a political arm of the Democratic Party, and the party was going to do what it could to oppose her. That meant the NAACP forbade Terrell from singing Kuhl's praises. The NAACP did not want him to endorse her even though he knew her to be a fair-minded judge and he thought she would be a great choice.

According to Terrell, two NAACP officials contacted him and told him to cease supporting Kuhl. Naturally, their request did not go over well with Terrell. He contacted Hannity and informed him of what was going on. Terrell was livid. The incident upset him so much that he resigned from the NAACP. Upon his resignation, he basically spilled the beans about how the NAACP is in the "back pocket" of the Democratic Party. The truthfulness and sincerity of Terrell, who had been so critical of Bush and the Republican Party, went a long way toward exposing the NAACP as a lap dog for the Democratic Party and straying far, far away from its original mission.

*

On October 1, 2004, Rush Limbaugh was basically forced to resign from ESPN for his comments about the Philadelphia Eagles' black quarterback, Donovan McNabb. The day after Limbaugh resigned from ESPN, I saw two staunch liberals defending Limbaugh on Fox News; Ellen Ratner and Alan Colmes. They did not agree with what Limbaugh had to say about McNabb, but they did not agree with ESPN's decision to let him go.

Without going into Limbaugh's comments, it was clear that the liberals, as in a lot of cases, rather than tolerating a conservative speaking out on issues that the liberals disagree with, simply wanted to take away the right for the conservative to speak. Basically, if you disagree, they want to shut you up rather than debate the issue. ESPN should not have caved in to liberals and forced Limbaugh to resign.

Take Senator Kerry, for instance. Rather than debate the swift-boat veterans about his service in Vietnam, Kerry threatened television stations with lawsuits if they ran the swift-boat vets' commercials. Then he tried to get their book taken off the bookshelves. If the swift-boat veterans were lying, he should have sued them, if he thought he had a case.

On the other hand, when Harry Belafonte called Dr. Condoleezza Rice and Colin Powell "house slaves," I did not see any black liberals defending Dr. Rice or Powell. Not even the NAACP stood up for these two fine blacks. Both Julian Bond and Kweisi Mfume were missing and could not stand up and say that while Dr. Rice and Powell may be Republicans, they are also black and are great role models for our youth.

As a black man, I find Limbaugh's opinion about the media to be far less meaningful than the fact that black people can accept our own calling two others "house slaves" and condoning it, only because they are of the opposite party.

*

In Atlanta, the nearby city of Stone Mountain was a haven for racism with J.B. Stoner, the Confederate flag, and the like. Basically, the only thing black people could do about the racism in Stone Mountain was stand on the periphery and talk about it. Then things began to change. Eventually, black people started moving to Stone Mountain. Lo and behold, so many blacks moved to Stone Mountain that the tides turned. In November 1997, the citizens of Stone Mountain voted in a black mayor!

My point is that we can do all the talking and criticizing on the outside, but once we get in and get involved, then we can make changes. Therefore, the Republican Party can be changed. But I also think that as more of us get into the Republican Party, we might find that it is not racist as some people would have us believe.

*

Over the years, I have come across several instances of the Democratic Party expecting black people to put the party ahead of their race. Attorney Vernadette Ramirez Broyles wrote about one such case in the *Atlanta Journal-Constitu-tion*. It had to do with Georgia's Democratic-controlled legislature's redrawing of the voting districts in the state. Broyles wrote about how the predominately white Democratic legislature drew the districts in a way that would benefit the party, all the while reducing black majorities in numerous districts, something that I do not agree with, anyway.

A three-judge federal panel rejected the map, stating that "it diluted minority voters' ability to elect minority candidates. However, the U.S. Supreme Court affirmed the original state Senate map, ruling that the ability of minorities to elect candidates of their choosing should no longer be the deciding factor in Voting Rights Act cases." The court felt that blacks may not necessarily have a majority black district where a black can almost be assured of being elected, but being that most blacks are Democrats, they at least can elect Democrats.

In short, the Democratic Party's powers-that-be put their party ahead of blacks.

Broyles, who is Latino, warns her own community about following the path of black voters by putting all their eggs in one basket. If they do so, she says, they "risk being reduced to mere political pawns."

*

Once President Bush took office, his appointments of blacks to prominent positions were great news to some. To others, particularly some fellow blacks, the appointments were perceived as bad news. Take Peter N. Kirsanow, for instance. In 2001, Bush appointed Kirsanow to the U.S. Civil Rights Commission. There was only one problem: Kirsanow is Republican. Mary Frances Berry, the commission's chairperson, tried practically everything she could to prevent Kirsanow from taking his position as part of the commission. She was putting the Democratic Party ahead of this black man seeking a position.

*

Is the party of blacks for all black candidates? I will point out cases where I think not, but you, the reader, can make up your own mind.

During the 2004 Democratic presidential primaries, Al Sharpton was initially the lone black candidate. Now Sharpton would not have been the black Democratic candidate of choice for me; with all the black Democrats in the country, the idea of Sharpton being the top black Democrat was comical. Was he the best black Democrats had to offer? I can think of numerous blacks who could have been elevated to presidential candidates.

With seven whites and one black candidate in the race for the Democratic nomination, the powers-that-be in the party seemed to grow concerned about votes being split up amongst the white candidates, leaving Sharpton with a sizeable amount. But so what? What if Sharpton had garnered more votes than the other candidates? The Democratic Party should not have had a problem with that, should it? Besides, the Democratic Party is the party of black minorities. The powers-that-be should not have had a problem with a black candidate whose race has 90 percent or more of its voters supporting their party. But that was not the case.

Here is what happened. In came Carol Moseley Braun, the former U.S. senator from Illinois. From all accounts, Braun had no aspirations of running for president. But being that Sharpton was the lone black Democratic candidate, the Democratic powers-that-be, including black Democratic strategist Donna Brazille, coaxed Moseley Braun into the race. But why? Could the reason have been to split up Sharpton's votes? I will leave it up to the reader to do the math.

Being the inquisitive person I am, I had a chance to ask Sharpton about this. On May 17, 2003, I attended the Black Expo Trade Show in Columbia, South Carolina. Sharpton had a booth in the trade show to promote his candidacy. After posing for photos with Sharpton, I said, "Reverend Sharpton, do you think Carol Moseley Braun was put in the race to split up your votes?" He said something to the effect that he had heard that but he did not know and he would have to see how things worked out. In my own opinion, Sharpton knew the game but he could not admit it.

Braun was not in attendance, but she did have a representative manning her booth. After speaking with Sharpton, I went to ask Braun's representative the same question. The booth volunteer said smilingly that she had not heard about Braun being put in the race to split up Sharpton's vote. I said, "Oh yeah? Well, you need to get in the know because that is the word that's going around."

Eventually, Sharpton's campaign lost the little steam it had. So after Braun's damage was done to Sharpton's chances of becoming a major player in the Democratic campaign, around November 4, 2003, Donna Brazille suggested that the bottom tier of candidates get out of the race—including both Sharpton and Braun. This was a stroke of genius for the Democratic officials—ridding the Democratic Party of its two black candidates. In my eyes, though, it was a stroke of disingenuousness.

Aside from this shenanigan by the Democratic officials, who could take Braun seriously after she was asked in a news conference what her college major was, and she could not recall?

It is quite telling that when it was advantageous for Democratic officials to put a black candidate in the presidential race to run against Sharpton, they did. But what about instances where they had opportunities to put black candidates in other races?

When it comes to an occasion for a person to be the first black or the first female to achieve a certain accomplishment, generally the female will be chosen. One case in point: The first American other than a white male to go into space was a female, Sally Ride, white no less. Later in 1983 came Guion "Guy" Bluford Jr., a black man. One side note: Air Force Major Robert H. Lawrence Jr., a test pilot, in 1967 became the first black astronaut. He was recognized posthumously by NASA at a ceremony on December 8, 1997, as the 17th astronaut to die while in training or on a mission into space. Major Lawrence flew many flights testing the gliding patterns of spacecraft returning to Earth from orbit.

In the case of politics, with all due respect to U.S. Congresswoman Shirley Chisholm—the first black woman elected to Congress, who campaigned unsuccessfully for the 1972 Democratic presidential nomination—the same thing occurred in the 1984 presidential race. Democratic presidential candidate Walter Mondale had an opportunity to select Jesse Jackson, a presidential candidate himself, as his vice-presidential running mate. Jackson would have been the first legitimate black vice-presidential running mate. This would have been a prime opportunity for the Democratic Party to throw a serious bone to its loyal black voters. And why not? Mondale did not stand a chance against incumbent President Reagan, especially after Mondale told America that he was going to raise taxes. So who did Mondale select? None other than Geraldine Ferraro, a white female.

The Mondale-Ferraro ticket went on to win a whopping one state, Mondale's home state of Minnesota, in the election against Reagan. Oh, and they also won Washington, D.C., a Democratic stranglehold—I mean stronghold. If they had selected Jackson, I imagine they would not have done any worse and might have done better, because Jackson stood a chance of winning his home state of South Carolina.

Another case in politics was when, in 2002, U.S. Senator Robert Torricelli was accused by the U.S. Senate of improperly accepting gifts. Torricelli read the tea leaves and figured that he could not win his re-election bid. Rather than go down in defeat to a Republican, Torricelli decided to bow out of the race. Or was he forced out by the New Jersey Democratic Party? Either way, it was past the legal deadline set by New Jersey law to replace him in the race. But why let a law get in the way of politics? The New Jersey Supreme Court saw fit to ignore the law and allowed the Democrats to replace Torricelli.

And who did the Democrats select to replace him? I say "replace" because the voters did not get an opportunity to vote on a replacement; it was left up to the New Jersey Democratic Party officials to select one. Trashing the law, did they take this opportunity to select a high-ranking black New Jersey official? Indeed not. They did not even select a woman this time. They chose retired Senator Frank Lautenberg, a white man of 70-plus years. Lautenberg had retired from the Senate because of his age. Unless he had found the Fountain of Youth during his retirement, he certainly hadn't gotten any younger. Surely the New Jersey Democratic Party could have found a black politician in New Jersey to replace him. After all, the Democratic Party is the party of blacks. Right?

Yet another case was in the state of Minnesota. On October 25, 2002, U.S. Senator Paul Wellstone, a Democrat, died in an airplane crash. He died during his re-election campaign, so the Democratic Party had to select a replacement to run in the U.S. senatorial race.

Minnesota Supreme Court Associate Justice Alan Page, a 57-year-old black man, reportedly had aspirations of replacing Wellstone on the ballot. From what I gathered, he was a well-qualified replacement. He has been on the Minnesota Supreme Court since 1993. Here yet again, with an opportunity to select a black man and throw black Democrats a bone for their loyalty, they instead chose another retired politician, the ever-popular, 70-plus-year-old Walter Mondale.

I have one more case and then I will quit. U.S. Senator Paul Coverdell of Georgia died in office on July 18, 2000. Governor Roy Barnes, a Democrat, was charged by the state's Constitution with replacing Coverdell. By now, you should now the outcome. This instance has to be one of the worst, though. Democrat Barnes not only did not choose this opportunity to throw a bone to the blacks of the state by selecting someone like former Atlanta mayor Maynard Jackson or another former Atlanta mayor and United Nations ambassador Andrew Young, he replaced Coverdell, a Republican, with a Democrat, former Governor Zell Miller. I recall Democrats, both statewide and nationwide, feeling ecstatic about this heartless decision. Looking back, though, it truly was a blessing in disguise. This time the Democrats' shenanigans backfired. Senator Miller proved to be one who puts his country above his party.

*

In each of the above cases, the Democratic Party could have used blacks in a positive manner but chose otherwise. But let us take a look at some instances of how they *did* use the black race.

Before the 2000 presidential election, I had an experience in my kids' elementary school that told me a lot about what kids learn at home. One afternoon, I went to pick up my kids from the after-school program. When I walked in the fifth-grade classroom, the kids and their teacher were having a discussion about George Bush and Al Gore. The teacher, assuming that I was a Democrat, wanted me to chime in on their discussion. I told the class that I was a Republican. Criticisms and questions began flying at me left and right from the students.

"Hold up, hold up," I said. "Let me take one student at a time."

One of the first questions I got was this: "Why do you like George Bush, he killed that man."

"What man?" I asked, thinking that this student had heard something that I had not heard.

"You know, the man in Texas," he said. Then he shockingly said, "He dragged that man's head off!"

I was flabbergasted—just absolutely floored! After hearing similar comments, I had to calmly explain to them what actually happened in Jasper, Texas, to James Byrd, Jr.

Later, after I left, I began to wonder where those children had gotten such erroneous information. I venture to say they got it from their parents and other relatives or, worse, picked it up from the NAACP television commercial that featured Byrd's daughter. In the commercial, the daughter stated that when Bush, as governor of Texas, failed to sign the hate-crime bill, it was like killing her father all over again. The commercial showed a pickup truck traveling down a road dragging a chain.

I had a lot of sympathy for Byrd's daughter then and still do, but I was appalled at the NAACP for encouraging her to participate in such a wrong-headed advertisement. This was a case in which a black was used to perpetuate the myth that Republicans are a bunch of racists. She unwittingly put the Democratic Party ahead of the truth.

When the three who actually committed the crime were sentenced in court, two were given the death penalty and the other, who cooperated with the authorities, received a sentence of life in prison. Now I have to ask, what more of a punishment could they have received under a hate-crime statute? Were hate-crime laws needed in this situation? I say no. Here are my thoughts on hate crimes. If someone is murdered, I can go out on a limb and say that the murderer hated the person he murdered or, at the very least, the murderer did not like that person. If a black man is murdered senselessly, his family more than likely will want the perpetrator of the crime arrested, found guilty, and given the maximum sentence—death even, if their state has the death penalty. The color of the perpetrator should not matter. It would not with me. I am not going to say, "Your Honor, being that it was a black-on-black crime, give the guilty one a life sentence," versus, "Your Honor, being that it was a white-on-black crime, give the guilty one the death penalty." Frankly, I want the stiffest sentence the law allows, regardless of the guilty person's color.

Another point is that if we truly looked at hate-crime laws, we would see they are counter to the Constitution. Proponents speak about violations of minorities' civil rights. The problem with this argument is that every citizen has civil rights—black, white, brown, or yellow. The hate-crime laws tend to separate us into categories of race—a road we should not want to travel.

Other NAACP-sponsored advertisements were despicable, too. The commercials stated that if Bush was elected president, more churches would burn. The sadness of this asinine statement was that, for the sake of the Democratic Party, the NAACP had blacks believing it.

During the height of the church burnings before the 2000 presidential election, President Clinton spoke up about how he recalled churches being burned in Arkansas. Apparently he was the only one who could recall this. The Little Rock newspaper researched this and did not come up with any church-burning incidents. Clinton was asked to apologize for his misstatement, but I am sure no one held his or her breath waiting on him.

*

In the aftermath of the 2000 presidential election, I found it appalling how blacks were being used by practically being accused of being too dumb to vote. Days after the election, I saw blacks complaining on C-SPAN that they had been unable to figure out the ballot. Some were saying they had been unable to punch out the chads.

Here is a quick lesson in voting, whether it is for individuals or issues: Do your homework before Election Day. Every time I go to the polling precinct to vote, there are voters trying to decide how to vote. During the 2000 election in Florida, copies of the butterfly ballot were printed in some of the newspapers. Next time, cut the sample ballot out of the newspaper, make your selections on it, and take it to the polling precinct.

There is something else I have noted that probably has been going on for some time. It is part of the dumbing-down of black voters. Rather than receiving detailed discussions of issues, we are given catch phrases or hooks, and then we are supposed to run with them. Jackson, who is known for this, gave us this ever-popular hook during the 2000 presidential election: "Stay out the Bushes. Stay out the Bushes." Then, after Bush won the election, Sharpton had to give us his own hook: "Bush was not e-lected, he was c-lected." It was like a rap freestyle battle between Jackson and Sharpton, as if they had to break the issue down to a level that blacks could understand.

Granted, there was some confusion with the butterfly ballot that was used in Florida. The saving grace for the Republicans was that the lady who designed the ballot, Theresa LePore, Palm Beach County elections supervisor, was a Democrat.

But I also throw in some divine intervention to explain Bush's victory.

A lot was said about the U.S. Supreme Court's two decisions on the 2000 presidential election. Here are their actual rulings:

In a 7-to-2 vote, the court held that the Florida Supreme Court improperly established new standards for resolving presidential election contests, thereby violating the Constitution, and that the state Supreme Court's order directing manual recounts without specific standards on how to review the ballots violated the Equal Protection Clause of the 14th Amendment.

The court further held, by a 5-to-4 majority, that federal election law specified a December 12 deadline for states to certify their winners, and that accordingly it was too late to allow any statewide recount remedy to proceed, even if the recount proceeded under the original standard. Basically, the Florida Supreme Court tried to usurp the state legislature and its laws, which is a no-no.

Some people ask about the hanging and dimpled chads. Let me explain with a baseball analogy. Have you ever gone to a major league game and picked up some all-star voting ballots? If there is a player you would really like to see in the Midsummer Classic, you can get a handful of ballots, stack them neatly, take a pointed object such as a pencil, and punch through the chads for your player. The ballots in the middle of the stack might have chads hanging on rather than punched all the way out. The ballots toward the back might have chads that are not hanging at all but merely dented, hence, the pregnant or dimpled chad. Get it?

As for the question of Gore and the popular vote, Bush was not the first president to lose the popular vote and win the election. He was the fourth to do so. Frankly, the popular vote does not mean a thing. Absolutely nothing! In presidential elections, what counts is the number of electoral votes that are accumulated.

Let me explain with a few sports analogies. In football, does it matter how many touchdowns (worth six points each) you get or how many field goals (worth three points each) you get? No coach or player will say, "The other team might have scored more points, but we scored more touchdowns!" Likewise, in baseball, does it matter how many grand slams (worth four runs) a team gets or how many bases-empty home runs a team gets? (Personally, I like the walk-off home run—a home run that wins a game.) Simply put, the popular vote does not mean jack!

What does mean something is the fact that Gore was the first candidate to lose his home state (in Gore's case, Tennessee) in the general election since George McGovern in 1972.

During the 2003 California gubernatorial election, Jackson complained in the media about blacks having problems voting. In essence, he was saying that blacks did not know how to vote. Jackson's complaining started before the election had even taken place. It was another instance of someone in the Democratic Party—in this case, Jackson—putting black people down in order to help the party.

For the history buffs, I will look a little farther back. Rather than fill the pages with reams of research, I will simply throw out a few topics and let you do your own research to see whether you come up with the conclusions that I allude to in this chapter:

President Woodrow Wilson, a Democrat, and his relationship with blacks.

- Alabama Governor George Wallace, a Democrat.
- Georgia Governor Lester Maddox, a Democrat.
- U.S. Senator James William Fulbright of Arkansas, avowed segregationist and Democrat. (By the way, Clinton claimed Senator Fulbright was his mentor.)

- South Carolina Democrat Governor Ernest Hollings and the Confederate flag that flew over the state capitol building. (It is funny how, during the 2000 presidential election, the Democrats all but said that Bush hoisted that flag atop the capitol building, never mentioning one word about Senator Hollings, a Democrat, who was in office when the flag was approved to fly above the capitol.)

*

Do you realize that, as a percentage, more Republicans than Democrats in the House and the Senate voted for the Civil Rights Act of 1964? Georgia Senator Richard B. Russell organized eighteen Southern Democratic senators in filibustering the bill. West Virginia Senator Robert C. Byrd, another Democrat, also filibustered the bill. By the way, he is a former Ku Klux Klansman, the only one I know of who is serving on the Hill.

My point is that there were and still are Democrats who are racists or bigots. I did not bring up examples of racist Republicans, not because there were or are none around today. It is just that we have been bombarded with a little truth and a lot of falsehood about Republicans and their stance on race.

We blacks never like to be stereotyped by whites saying, "Ya'll look alike." But what about when all of us think or vote alike? Should we be appalled at that? I certainly think so, but it is quite apparent that not all blacks have the same sentiments I do.

*

Supreme Court Justice Clarence Thomas draws criticism from many so-called black leaders and black media outlets. Why? Because he is a conservative. They are of the opinion that if a black is not liberal and a supporter of the Democratic Party, he or she is a sell-out to the black race. If Thomas does not put a liberal spin on his court decisions, they consider him to be betraying his race.

I have seen Thomas being interviewed and asked what guides him in his court decisions. He states that the Constitution guides him and gives him his foundation when deciding cases and writing opinions. He is what is called an originalist, believing in the original meaning of the Constitution. Personally, I see nothing wrong with that.

However, in Thomas' critics' view, you cannot be a constitutionalist and be supportive of blacks. They want him to rule one way for blacks and another way for everyone else. But what about Justice Thurgood Marshall? Marshall used the Constitution to strike down unconstitutional laws in our country—the very same Constitution that Thomas uses.

What about redrawing voting districts to get more blacks in a district, thus assuring that a black will be elected in that district? Not surprisingly, Thomas disagrees with redistricting on the basis of race. He wrote, "Our drive to segregate political districts by race can only serve to deepen racial divisions by destroying any need for voters or candidates to build bridges between racial groups." How right he is in this opinion. In other words, if a district's racial makeup is 50 percent black and 50 percent white, the elected officials will have to cater to the needs of all the citizens of that district or risk being voted out. The elected officials will be compelled to build bridges between the races. But if the district is redrawn to make the racial makeup 95 percent one race and 5 percent the other, the elected officials will more than likely be of the race with the 95 percent. Thus, the elected officials might be less inclined to build a bridge between the races. The officials might be more inclined to build walls between the races.

A prime example is Congresswoman Cynthia McKinney of

Georgia. With her district being majority black, she not only has put up walls to rival the Great Wall of China, she has even dug trenches militaries would be proud to have.

I must say I wholeheartedly agree with Thomas on redrawing districts for the purpose of getting a particular race elected. Besides, what other characteristics should we divide districts by: age, gender, sexual preferences? Whatever the makeup of the district, that district will have to elect someone, and hopefully that person can bridge the gaps among all groups.

Then there is Thomas' view on affirmative action. Perhaps Thomas did benefit from affirmative action by getting into college. Frankly, I do not know. But for argument's sake, let us say he did. Could it be that, over the years, he has learned about affirmative action and its negative effects on an individual or on a race? Haven't we all been in agreement or disagreement with an issue and, after further review, had a change of heart?

*

What about conservative blacks? According to NAACP President Kweisi Mfume, speaking in July 2004, "Conservative black organizations are formed and funded by white Republicans." He went on to say, "They can't deal with the leaders we choose for ourselves, so they manufacture, promote, and hire new ones." Sadly, this was in an address to the NAACP Convention. Surely there are conservatives in the NAACP. Besides, I do not recall an election to choose leaders for our race. If there was an election, I would like a recall.

As I mentioned in the first chapter, I am aware of "black slate" fliers, though until the 2004 elections, I had not seen one in a while. During that year's election primaries in Clayton County, Georgia, a "Palm Card to take to the polls" was sent out in the mail to some Clayton County citizens. Since I live in Clayton County, I received one. It was sent out by a group called "The July 20, 2004 Ballot of Concerned Afro-Americans; Citizens of Clayton County." At least, that is what was in the return address section of the card. The Palm Card listed nine "Black candidates and incumbents in contested elections that deserve our vote and support!" The Coalition of Black Christian Clergy, claiming to represent many of the community's churches, endorsed all of the candidates.

I am not sure how all nine candidates fared in the election, but I do know that, thankfully, the black voters did not re-elect two particular candidates simply because they were black. In 2003, the Southern Association of Colleges and Schools placed the Clayton County school system on probation and threatened to revoke the system's accreditation after three incumbents—the two blacks and a white—were the focus of allegations of board micromanagement of the school system.

*

On July 25, 2003, President Bush nominated Janice Rogers-Brown to the U.S. Court of Appeals for the District of Columbia Circuit. Rogers-Brown, who is black, had been an associate justice on the California Supreme Court since 1996. Blacks should be proud of Bush for proving others wrong about his alleged dislike of blacks. But that isn't the case. In October 2003, I heard Tavis Smiley on the radio telling black people where we should stand in regard to Rogers-Brown. Hardly anyone around the country had ever heard of her and very few people knew how she had ruled in court cases. But rather than ask black people to do their own research on Rogers-Brown, Smiley told us that she was not the one for us. He went on to denigrate her for her court decisions as if she was anti-black. It seems it is okay for blacks to disapprove of someone because of his or her beliefs, but influential blacks take their marching orders from the Democratic Party and then tell the rest of black America where we should stand. I have a problem with that.

Why are we blacks not charged with doing our own homework on issues, topics, and individuals? After doing so, we could make up our own minds. If we all come to the same conclusions, so be it. I, in fact, did my homework on Rogers-Brown and came to the opposite conclusion of Smiley. It was just another case where we as blacks were all supposed to think alike in an effort to help the Democratic Party.

*

On October 18, 2003, I purchased Larry Elder's book *The Ten Things You Can't Say in America.* I only had to read as far as the Preface page, page number xi, before he made a point that was evident in an article from the *Atlanta Journal-Constitution.*

Elder states that, "The well-intentioned though wrong-headed 'war against poverty' ... actually encourages poverty." On October 17, 2003, an article in the paper by Patricia Guthrie was titled, "Food stamp publicity boosts rolls." The article was basically about how the Georgia Department of Human Resources' Division of Family and Children Services, known as DFCS, was helping "more poor people use the federally funded food stamp program resulted in a 13 percent increase in enrollment for fiscal year 2002." In other words, the state had performed outreach efforts to get more people dependent on the federal program. One way they had reached out was by printing eligibility requirements on grocery bags.

To top this off, the article went on to state that, "DFCS expects to be presented with an award for its efforts next month at the annual food stamp directors' conference in Nevada."

Does something seem awry here? Should it not be the government's job to *lessen* the number of people dependent upon it? If that were the case, should not there be an award for *reducing* enrollment and making people less dependent on the government?

*

There are a number of issues on which the Democratic Party is at odds with many black people. The issue of school vouchers is one of these. We all know of the poor quality of the educations that a lot of black students receive, especially in poor black neighborhoods. We also know about the debate over school vouchers. My thought is that if the schools are failing and the black kids are failing, we must try something different. I am not alone in my support of vouchers, because as surveys and polls show, more than half of blacks support them.

By now, we should all know that the solution is not more money. Still, there are some, particularly those in the teachers' unions, who try to persuade us that more money will solve the problem. But the crux of the problem is the teachers' unions themselves for refusing to go along with school vouchers. For some reason, they do not want the competition. But they do support the Democratic Party with money and votes. Therefore, the Democratic Party will not support school vouchers. Once again, blacks are asked to put the party ahead of black kids and their education.

When it comes to education, does the Democratic Party really want its constituents to get a great education? After all, the Democrats say that the Republican Party is for the rich. We all know that, by and large, the more education one obtains, the more income one is apt to make. Put simply, more education equals more money equals Republican Party. So it could be that the Democrats do not want black kids to get a better education. At least, that is the way I see it when they say the Republican Party is for the rich.

Imagine that you are a new immigrant to this country, having arrived penniless. Then you are told that once you become a citizen, you should join a political party. If you are told that the Democratic Party is for the poor and the Republican Party is for the rich, which would you want to join? Personally, I would want to join the party of the rich! Sign me up with the party that will help me achieve the rich status, not the party that will fight to keep people dependent on the government.

I have one other point on this matter. Imagine the members of a poor black family, all of whom have been life-long Democrats. One day, they hit the jackpot in the lottery and become instant multimillionaires. As soon as they cash the first check, the Democratic Party, its policies, and its rhetoric will be against that family, merely because of their newfound financial status. They might still want to support the Democratic Party, but as soon as they get the new big-screen television hooked up, they will see Democrats all over the screen denigrating rich people. It is funny how this happens, because I know there are rich people in the Democratic Party, especially on Capitol Hill!

Another issue about which the Democratic Party and many black people disagree is same-sex marriage. The Democratic Party is highly in favor of gay marriage. For the most part, blacks are against this type of union.

Case in point: In March 2004, in Georgia, approximately thirty black pastors signed a declaration against same-sex marriage. This was in response to the Democratic state representatives' opposition to a state constitutional ban on same-sex marriage. Here again, the black Democratic representatives put their party over the race.

Conflicts like these will continue to pop up in the Democratic Party more often than in the Republican Party. The reason is that the Democratic Party invites any and everyone, regardless of their stance on issues, into its big tent. The party says, "Whatever your beliefs are, come on in. We will sort out the differences later." Pretty soon, the tent is overflowing with tree-huggers as well as land developers; Christians as well as gays who believe in same-sex marriage; PETA members, vegans and pig farmers; poor blacks as well as rich blacks; and peaceniks as well as military veterans, all with their own agendas. But when it comes to what direction the occupants of the tent are going to go when they get their marching orders, that is another story.

Republicans, on the other hand, post their stances on issues on the door of their tent and say, "If you agree with these stances, come on in." The above mentioned groups can also be found in the Republican Party, but when they get their marching orders, they are basically headed in the same direction. That is because, for the most part, the different groups in the Republican Party tent leave their personal agendas at the door.

Why is it that black people form the only race that pledges its allegiance to one party? Hispanics, Asians, Arabs, and whites are in both major political parties. It is well past the time that black people diversify when it comes to political parties. We need to take a closer look at the Republican Party.

8

Conservative Politics 101

I have heard that it is easy to be a Democrat. To be a Republican, though, is much harder. The primary reason is that, to be a Republican, you have to educate yourself. There is no specific way to educate yourself, but I will give some recommendations and tell you about some of the things I did to educate and reprogram myself.

*

First, I expanded my news and information sources. This was essential because of the prevalent liberal bias in the media.

I am sure my experience as a child absorbing the news and current events was similar to most everyone's. We are all students of the media, with some being more studious than others. Initially, you perhaps think that whatever comes on the news is true and accurate. I think that, because I was a student, my first thoughts on the news were about where the news came from. I don't mean the news events themselves. I wondered whether there was something like a warehouse where all the news stories went to be disseminated.

As I got older, I wondered how it was that I could dial through about six television channels and see practically the same news stories on all the news shows everyday. I thought that with all the news that goes on around the country and the world, surely ABC's news should be different from CBS's and NBC's. But if I watched one at 7 p.m. and watched another at 7:30 p.m., they would have virtually the same news stories. This really intrigued me, even at a young age.

I eventually learned about the Associated Press and the Reuters News Agency, how they basically have teams of reporters and how a news story reported by either one of these companies is shared with media outlets. Still, this did not explain how each media outlet selected the same news stories and sometimes broadcast them in practically the same order. At one point in my young life, I thought there was a man, white no doubt, deciding what got aired on the news.

After being educated over the years by liberal-leaning news anchors and reporters such as Walter Cronkite, Peter Jennings, Tom Brokaw, Katie Couric, and Bryant Gumbel, and by media outlets such as ABC, CBS, NBC, CNN, the *Washington Post*, and the *Atlanta Constitution*, just to name some of the popular ones, I found that there were other individuals and media outlets that had different points of view. Over time, I have discovered a plethora of alternative sources.

My first memory of media manipulation and bias had to do with future Major League Baseball Hall of Famer Rickey Henderson. Henderson broke Lou Brock's all-time base-stealing record of 938 on May 1, 1991. He had the reputation of being a hot-dog type of player and of being self-centered. I had always admired him as a player, though. More recently, when he was with the New York Mets, I saw him play against the Atlanta Braves. Fans loved to get on Henderson and try to pluck his nerves.

On that day in 1991, I was watching the evening news and channel surfing. One of the big three news stations replayed Henderson's comments after he stole the record-breaking base. The umpires stopped the game. Henderson held up the bag and spoke briefly but glowingly of Lou Brock by saying, "Lou Brock certainly was a symbol of great base stealing, but today, I am the greatest of all time." After channel surfing, I saw the same news clip. Only this time, they left out Henderson's praise of Brock! They merely showed Henderson holding up the stolen base and stating, "I am the greatest of all time." This somewhat minor example of media bias and manipulation of someone's speech was very enlightening.

Another incident happened here in Atlanta during a 2000 presidential debate. Former local political reporter Bill Nigut was doing a news segment about the debate. When he replayed Al Gore's comments, he included the audience's applause for Gore. The audience actually gave George Bush a bigger round of applause in response to one of his comments, but WSB left most of the applause clip on the cutting-room floor. This is another example of media bias and manipulation that clearly shows that sometimes we do not get the truth or the full story from the media.

As I noted earlier, one major way I expanded my news and information sources was by listening to talk radio. Granted, not all talk shows are alike, but the benefit I derived from talk radio was the sheer coverage of so many issues, political and otherwise. Fortunately, I got to listen to some of the best in the country, giants such as Neal Boortz, Rush Limbaugh, and Sean Hannity. I would put Kim Peterson of radio station

WGST of Atlanta in that category, mainly because he is a true patriot of this country.

Sometimes I agree with a talk show host and sometimes I do not. If I disagree with a host on a particular issue, that does not mean I will never listen to him again. Many people call or write hosts to say they will no longer listen because they have disagreements. That is the wrong approach. I will say, though, that if you disagree with a host most of the time, you probably should change the dial.

Listening to talk radio gave me a chance to hear myriad sides to any number of issues. By hearing so many viewpoints, I got to make up my own mind on how I felt about the issues. On some issues, my stance was forged by listening to talk radio. On other issues, I did a 180-degree turn on my stance, mainly because I gathered more information. Then there were issues on which I had no stance at all. If I chose to formulate a stance, I listened and gathered information on the issue and decided what suited me.

Newspapers are a great source of information, even though most papers are liberal-leaning. I can at least use the newspapers to make comparisons with the reports I get from news outlets I use. When reading newspapers, you must be able to distinguish the news stories, which should be factual; the editorials, which are written by members of the editorial board of the newspaper; and the opinion columns, which are merely opinions of the various writers. A great thing about newspapers is that most are posted on the Internet.

Speaking of the Internet, it has revolutionized information gathering. There is a plethora of Web sites, such as townhall.com and jewishworldreview.com, where you can read columnists' opinions about current issues and events. Do not let the jewishworldreview.com name fool you—some of the best columnists can be found on that Web site.

For the longest time, television news has been liberal-leaning. National news outlets ABC, CBS, NBC, and later CNN were and still are very supportive of the Democratic Party. But few people understood this for many years. Limbaugh was one of the few who did, and he was happy to point it out to us "ditto heads."

Television news has been transformed since the mid-1990s. Limbaugh's television show was groundbreaking, but the advent of Fox News has had perhaps the greatest effect. Critics label Fox News as conservative. Because other networks have virtually no conservative voices, and because Fox puts on both conservative and liberal voices, it *does* seem conservative. I say more power to Fox News, because conservative as well as liberal voices and opinions need to be heard.

Secondly, I immersed myself in the founding documents of our country. Actually, if I were starting over, I would start with this first, because learning about our country's beginning and reading what our Founding Fathers said and wrote at the time gives you the best foundation. You don't have to agree with everything the Founding Fathers wrote, but you should at least know the beginning history of the country.

I found reading and studying about our country's history not just educational but rewarding. I read about Thomas Paine pumping up George Washington's troops and the citizens of our Colonies with his pamphlet *Common Sense*. I discovered how Benjamin Franklin, as our ambassador to France, was one our country's original players—or playboys, as some would say. He charmed the ladies of Paris so they would convince their men to aid the Colonies' quest for independence. Surprisingly, I found I had not forgotten everything I had learned in school. In fact, I melded what I had previously learned with the knowledge I was gaining.

Another way I increased my information sources was through books. In January 1997, I went to a book signing by Star Parker. Her book is titled *Pimps, Whores and Welfare*

Brats: From Welfare Cheat to Conservative Messenger. Parker's book is about her life of crime, drugs, and welfare among other negatives, and how she had to fight to get off the welfare treadmill. She also exposes racism pimps such as Jesse Jackson. Her book was truly an eye-opener for me. I recommend it to everybody—black, white, rich, or poor. We all can benefit from it. I mention some of the other helpful books I read in Chapter 8 and Chapter 12.

Another important step was learning about the origins and history of the Republican Party. For too long, the Republican Party has been defined by its opposition, the Democratic Party. Basically, the Democrats have been telling us the positions and stances of the Republican Party. That is like having one of your friends tell you about someone else you might want to befriend. The two of them might be the worst of enemies, but that does not mean you and the potential friend cannot get along.

Here is a prime example of how Democrats have defined Republicans. Democrats claim that the Republican Party and its members are racist. I must say they even had me believing this claim. But when I started doing my homework on the Republican Party, I discovered differently. I found that the Republican Party was formed as an anti-slavery party in response to the Kansas-Nebraska Act, passed by Congress in 1854, which permitted slavery in the new territories of Kansas and Nebraska. The party was formed because some members of the Whig Party wanted to continue the institution of slavery. Learning this was truly an eye-opener for me.

After all of that, I had to learn about the Republican Party's stances on political issues. The funny thing is that blacks and Republicans agree on a lot of issues. However, as I said, the Republican Party has been labeled as racist by its opposition, and because the opposition can use the mainstream media to get that falsehood out to the public, it is a hard lie to combat.

*

During the Racial Reconciliation Forum in Atlanta in October 2003, someone asked why Georgia Governor Sonny Perdue, a Republican, had appointed so few minorities to his administration and other positions. We blacks cannot have it both ways. If the majority of blacks are in the Democratic Party, it is hard to complain with any validity when the pool of black Republicans is so small. It was not a matter of appointing blacks or whites for Perdue or for any of our previous governors; it was a matter of appointing people of their own party. I do not recall former Georgia Governors Roy Barnes or Zell Miller appointing many Republicans—black or white.

During the past few years, I have been asked a few times why I am a Republican. The short answer is I have discovered I have conservative beliefs. Moreover, I have found that when your beliefs are conservative, you tend to vote with the Republican Party because the Republican Party is conservative. Some people would say that a conservative and a Republican are one and the same. That is not necessarily true. Supposedly, there are conservative Democratic politicians. There are also Republican politicians who could be called liberals. Actually, I think it is impossible to be liberal and a Republican. But who knows? So many of today's politicians couch themselves and regularly redefine their affiliation titles that you cannot truly pin down their party beliefs.

The way to figure out whether you are liberal or conservative is to do your homework. Establish some core beliefs of your own and do not vacillate like so many people do. Once your core beliefs are established, you will be able to recognize when a politician or a party veers from what you believe. Then you will be able to make an intelligent decision as to whether you should continue to support that individual or party.

Democrats seem to lack core principles. Whatever side of

an issue Bush comes down on, the Democratic Party takes the other side for the sake of disagreement. This can happen only when you do not have core beliefs.

Take Senator John Kerry, for instance. Kerry stated that he would like to see some of our troops around the world brought home. A month or so later, when Bush said virtually the same thing, Kerry disagreed. He at least could have said that the president was stealing his ideas.

The Republican Party is strong on defense issues, and I wholeheartedly agree with the party. During the times that we live in, I am a staunch believer in pre-emptive strikes on terrorists. We cannot sit back and wait until we are attacked and then retaliate as some would have us to do. We have been down that road, and it is not pretty.

September 11, 2001, was a tragic day, one that I was reminded of every morning when I worked at Marsh USA Inc. On that day, a co-worker by the name of Maynard Spence was visiting our company offices in the World Trade Center. Our company had offices located roughly on the 92nd through 100th floor in the North Tower. On that day, Spence and 294 other colleagues died a horrible death. Roughly 10 percent of the deaths that day were company colleagues of mine. The Marsh office in Atlanta has a memorial in honor of Spence that I passed by every workday. May God bless all the victims of September 11, 2001.

So terrorism in this country and around the world is not something I take lightly. I try to heed the advice of the Department of Homeland Security—I *stay* on orange, if not on red alert everyday.

Sadly though, some people act as if the terrorist strikes of September 11, 2001, did not happen. How can people talk about the number of jobs lost since Bush took office without considering that many jobs were lost due to the attacks?

It is even sadder when people here in Atlanta say the same

thing, knowing that Atlanta's economy was affected drastically. After all, Atlanta is a convention city. On September 11, 2001, I was attending a convention that eventually closed down early, hurting Atlanta's economy within hours of the attacks. Shortly after, other conventions were cancelled. Of course, we all know how busy Atlanta's Hartsfield-Jackson International Airport is year round. There is no telling how much revenue was lost at the airport when the airspace was closed after the attacks. All of this deleteriously affected Atlanta's economy, yet people right here in this city refuse to acknowledge the September 11 attacks. Go figure.

9

Recommendations
on Some Major Issues

—◄•►—

$\mathbf{A}$s I have thought through my political beliefs, I have
formulated positions on a host of social issues. Here
are my recommendations for addressing some pressing problems.

Education

Growing up in North Carolina, it was always exciting to listen
on the radio to the football scores of the black college games.
The sheer number of black schools was astounding. Back in
the day, a great many of the Historically Black Colleges and
Universities (HBCU) were powerhouses in sports, as well as
in academics.

The HBCUs were founded to give black people places of
higher learning at a time when they were not allowed to fur-

ther their learning at many colleges and universities. Since their establishment, a countless number of black people have graduated from some fine colleges and universities.

Over the years, however, many HBCUs have fallen on hard times. Enrollment has decreased, as well as financial support. Also, the sports programs' level of competitiveness has decreased. The integration of the predominately white schools has left HBCUs with a challenge to recruit black college-eligible students.

Speaking of college-eligible students, I have heard countless times that there are more black people in jail than in college. That might be true overall. However, the statisticians throw out the age factor. When you compare the number of kids in college against the number of college-age people in prison, I doubt that the mantra holds true.

My recommendations are three-fold. First, beef up the academic programs at the HBCUs. One way to do this is to have a professor recruitment drive. Just as there has been a coming-home of blacks moving back to the South, so black professors can be challenged to join HBCUs. This will bode well for attracting the brightest black students.

Second, beef up the sports programs and their facilities. Start with the basketball teams because they have only twelve players each, so it would not be as costly as beefing up football teams with their greater number of players, not to mention the cost of uniforms and facilities. HBCUs can recruit top-level basketball coaches, whether they are experienced coaches or retired NBA players. Yes, the black coaches and NBA players can come home also, just like the professors.

Once the facilities are up to par and the black coaches are in place, a recruitment drive can be started to bring the best players in the country to the HBCUs. Once this happens, ESPN and other sports networks will begin knocking on the doors of HBCUs to televise their games. And this, after all, is what top athletes want—national television time! Imagine Dick Vitale and ESPN at the Central Intercollegiate Athletic Association's annual basketball tournament. They would not be able to get enough of Mr. CIAA, a fan from Virginia who has been attending the tournament for decades I imagine. He casually struts through the arena dressed in outfits of the different team's colors. Never heard of him? Wait until the networks get of hold of him. Finally, we as blacks must put aside our party affiliations and begin to support school vouchers. Sure, every child may not get a voucher, but at least they would help some kids who are mired in failing schools. Supporting school vouchers will help some kids get better educations, which will turn out more college-eligible students. Let us remember who the opponents of school vouchers are. As I said before, teacher unions are against vouchers. Teacher unions support the Democratic Party. Hence, the Democratic Party will be against school vouchers. You do the math—or the trigonometry, if you have used a school voucher.

Affirmative action

Affirmative action has opponents and proponents. There are so-called experts who claim to have the answers to the problems of affirmative action. Well, I am no expert, but I have an opinion that I would like to share.

President Nixon, a Republican, of course, initiated the Philadelphia Order, which was a plan to guarantee fair-hiring practices for construction jobs in Philadelphia. Apparently Nixon was not the Republican racist a lot of black people think he was. Still, while he may have had good intentions, there are problems.

First, should affirmative-action programs help any and all blacks or only poor blacks? Frankly, I say that if benefits and/ or money should assist any person, it should be poor people.

Take a hypothetical example. King High School, located in a poverty-stricken city, has seventy-five seniors: twenty-five blacks, twenty-five whites, and twenty-five Hispanics. The families of all of these students are living in government housing and on welfare. All the students score 950 on their SATs. Come college acceptance time, the black and Hispanic students get an additional 25 points on their college entrance exams because of their race. Consequently, they get accepted to Davidson County Community University. The white students do not get accepted because their 950 SAT scores are not high enough. Come on, affirmative-action proponents: Does this seem fair to the white kids?

Here's another hypothetical example. World Computer Company, located in Atlanta, has five departments and two hundred employees: 180 whites and twenty blacks. The five departments all have white department heads who are in charge of hiring for their respective departments. Of the last forty employees hired, all have been college graduates and white. Of the last thirty employees promoted within the company, all have been white, save for one black employee.

Come on, affirmative-action opponents: Does this seem fair to the black employees? Sure, this scenario does not cover all of the specifics of employment, but if the black employees are not qualified to be promoted, how is it they are qualified to be hired?

My recommendation? First, get rid of this affirmative-action notion. Affirmative action connotes admitting students to colleges and universities or hiring people because of the mere fact that they are black, qualifications notwithstanding. This stigma is one that most blacks, and certainly I, would not want.

Let us look at Arthur Ashe's comments on affirmative action in his book titled *Days of Grace*. Ashe wrote, "Practically, affirmative action is probably necessary. But I would not want to know that I received a job simply because I am black. Affirmative action tends to undermine the spirit of individual initiative. Such is human nature; why struggle to succeed when you can have something for nothing!"

With that said, let me give a few examples and comments regarding affirmative action.

As most black and white people will tell you, America is not 100 percent purged of discrimination, bigotry, or racism. These problems are not near the levels they once were, but there is one way that they still persist. I have said for the longest time that blacks should go into the business of job-training because, across America, particularly in corporate America, there are countless cases of a black employee training a newly hired or recently transferred white employee, only to see the white employee be moved into the black employee's position or promoted over that black employee. This is wrong. It is as if the black employee lacks something that the white employee has obtained, or perhaps has something that the white employee does not—blackness. I have personally seen this scenario played out far too many times while working in corporate America.

Some people would deny this is a problem. They say the company wants to hire and promote the employees who will help the bottom line the most, regardless of color. This is not necessarily true because, in corporate America, many jobs are far removed from the bottom line and do not directly affect it in the way a salesperson or a salaried worker can. This deleterious and discriminatory pattern may not be as common in small businesses because the employees, regardless of their position, are closer to the bottom line and the employer looks closer at what each employee contributes to the company.

Leonard Pitts, a columnist with the *Miami Herald* newspaper, enlightened me through one of his columns that some whites get promoted or hired through their own affirmative-action program. When only white college graduates are hired and only white employees are properly trained and then promoted, this is affirmative action for them.

This is not a Republican- or Democratic-led phenomenon, either. In workplaces where I have seen this firsthand, some of the black employees would try to put the onus on the Republican company leaders. However, I imagine that there are just as many Democratic office heads and department managers as there are Republicans.

My recommendations: First, office managers and department managers of corporate America should take a walk around their companies—floor to floor, in each department—and see where the black employees are concentrated. In all too many companies, they will find that most of their black employees are concentrated in the service departments: mailroom workers, janitorial staff, word-processing specialists, receptionists, building maintenance workers, assistants to the sales staff, and so forth. If this is true, that office or department manager needs to make a concerted effort to recruit qualified blacks.

Second, ensure that black employees who are currently employed are properly trained, making them eligible to be promoted.

Finally, recruit qualified blacks from the local colleges. If the company is located in a city that has colleges, particularly black colleges, make a concerted effort to recruit black students from these schools. Recruiters can hire the cream of the crop of qualified black students from these colleges.

If a college is located in a predominately white city or state, more than likely the student population will be predominately white. There is nothing inherently wrong with this situation. But it would be wrong for the college to recognize this and then try to recruit black students for the sake of diversity so that the white kids could gain some type of experience by sitting in class with black students.

If a college is located in a city or state with a substantial black population and that college has few black students, it should work with the city or state to recruit qualified black students. If the pool of qualified black students is dismal, the college can work to get black kids prepared and qualified by establishing mentoring programs with the local schools, from the elementary schools to the high schools. Most colleges want as many students as can fit in their system. After all, colleges are in the business of teaching and making money. Why not prepare kids to be potential students for their college?

Can you imagine the Georgia Institute of Technology and Emory University, both excellent schools of higher learning in Atlanta, competing to see who can mentor the most kids and eventually enroll them? They could pattern their programs after the methods some schools use to recruit athletes. The pitch might go something like this: "Hey, little Tyrone, sign up for Georgia Tech's mentoring program and we can get you the best calculator on the market. Need a laptop computer? We can get you a wireless one so when you go to your fifth-grade class, you can be mobile!" Or: "Hey Tameka Jackson, sign up with Emory's Each-One-Teach-One program and we can get you a 'dope' dictionary and a 'tight' thesaurus for your eighth-grade class. Then you can learn to replace *dope* with *extraordinary* and *tight* with *stupendous*."

With all the good-hearted people in America, blacks, whites, and others, we can really make some positive changes in education and the workplace.

Ideally, you want to hire the best person for the job, regardless of race or gender. But sometimes there is no way of determining who is the best person for the job. Take hiring a coach for a professional football team. With so many candidates, there is no way to say that one individual is the best.

If 90 percent of the players on an NFL team are black, human nature might compel the players to say, "Yes, we can be coached by a white individual, but if 90 percent of us are black and can play the game, why can't a black person coach the game?" Often, in situations such as coaching, it comes down to who can gain the respect of the team.

Case in point: the Dallas Cowboys. They seemed to have grown accustomed to losing—until Bill Parcells was hired. His reputation of being a proven winner preceded him. Because of that, he instantly had a lot of respect from the players. Consequently, the Cowboys began to win in his first year at the helm. Mind you, Parcells is white, but he brought experience as well as success to the table.

Black coaches, by and large, can bring experience, stick-to-itiveness, and a will and desire to succeed through perseverance. There are numerous black coaches who have been in the trenches of coaching, learning and honing their craft without a shot at a head coaching position. But when the time comes for one of those coaches, players, black and white, can look in that coach's eyes and say, "I respect you because of your determination and willingness to hang in there after getting passed over so many times. Therefore, I am going to show my respect to you by playing my heart out for you."

Sometimes, in situations such as coaching where black coaches are so rare, when one is finally selected to coach, a lot of respect is afforded that individual for several reasons. One is that there is a kindred spirit between blacks, whose forefathers were perhaps shut out of a particular field of work.

That is why the selection of the first black coach in a particular sport or a special accomplishment by one of them frequently is looked upon as a victory not just for that individual but for the race. Understandably, this does not resonate with all white people. This is not a knock on white people; it is just something that white people, for the most part, do not experience. At the same time, it is no knock on blacks that they feel a sense of accomplishment when the first black this or the first black that occurs.

Hiring a *qualified* black—and let me reiterate, a qualified black and not merely a token black—for a prominent position in coaching or corporate America sends a message to everyone in that organization. It says, "We hire qualified individuals, regardless of color." Hiring a qualified black in a company also could send a positive message to the employees, especially to the black employees, causing them to say to themselves, "If I work diligently and become qualified for a particular position, I have an opportunity to get that position." And it causes the white employees to say to themselves, "I should not rely on my race to get a job or promotion." This, in turn, will cause them to work diligently as well to climb the ladder of success.

Such a hiring and promoting policy makes everyone work harder for the company, which only helps that company's productivity. Thus, it is a win-win situation for the employees of all races of that company and the company itself.

Some companies get a reputation for being unfair to blacks, whites, or other segments of society in their hiring process. Yes, unfair to whites, too. There are black-owned companies that discriminate against whites. But imagine if a company has a reputation for hiring and promoting people regardless of race or gender. After all, some people refrain from seeking employment at certain companies or government offices whose unfair promotion or hiring processes are unbecoming. It seems to me that the best potential employees would flock to a company whose reputation is upstanding with all races.

Black groups

One bone of contention between blacks and whites is the existence of black organizations, events, and groups such as Miss Black America, BET, Black Farmers of America, and so on.

There is nothing wrong with these things. At the same time, it would be okay to have a Miss White America pageant. Some would say that there already is one—the Miss America pageant—but I disagree. The First Amendment to the Constitution gives us the right to freely associate. In saying this, we blacks cannot get upset at all-white groups or all-male groups such as the Augusta National Country Club.

Growing up seeing very few blacks on television, a number of us hoped for a black television station where all the shows would be about black people: sitcoms, dramas, news shows, everything. Hence, Black Entertainment Television (BET). But who envisioned it being a music-video station. But we cannot get mad at BET's founder, Bob Johnson, for the station's programming. The remote works on BET just like on the other stations. We can be disappointed, though. My recommendation: People of different races should not get upset at other races for establishing groups, associations, or businesses, particularly if they are legal and especially if they are positive endeavors.

Tax savings

When rich Democrats talk about the tax cuts that President Bush passed, time and again they say that they and other rich people do not need the money.

My recommendation: Use your tax money to help out a family or person in need. When you get a tax cut, do not act as if you must blow that money. There are several charitable causes to which people can contribute their tax money if they choose to do so. I think letting taxpayers keep more of their money and cutting out the middleman (government) is a better solution when it come to helping others.

Song lyrics

What's up with our music? Some of the lyrics of today's songs are akin to the acts of Redd Foxx, Rudy Ray Moore, or Millie Jackson. Adults, including my parents, bought these performers' records to listen to themselves, not to play for us kids. And we certainly did not hear such content over the black, community-conscious radio station airwaves. When these adult records were played by our parents, my siblings and I were sent outside or to our rooms, where we had to shut the door. Even if we did hear some of what was being said on these records, the fact that our parents made us shut the doors to our rooms was like putting up barriers between adult material and us. The shutting of the doors said, "This is not for you." Nowadays, however, these types of lyrics and language are geared to young kids, teenagers, and young adults.

I do like the tight beats and some of the hooks in today's music, particularly rap or hip-hop. After all, most of it is recycled from my growing-up years. I certainly also like to dance. I just have to separate the lyrics from the beats. Earth, Wind and Fire sang, "Keep your head to the sky," while 50 Cent sings, "I don't look to the sky no more." I like 50's CD, but is it for my 15- and 13-year-old kids? I think not. But there are far more 15- and 13-year-olds who own 50 Cent's CD than 45-year-old adults.

During my childhood, my family would occasionally gather in the living room, put on some 45-rpm records, and dance and sing away. Can we 40-plus people conceive of dancing and singing with our parents and grandparents to songs proclaiming "I love to pump crack," "Smoking some buds," or "I'll kill you"? Compare Curtis Mayfield's "Fred is dead" to songs that talk about selling "fat pillows" (nickel and dime bags of weed).

In the '60s and '70s, there was black music that pretty much catered to all ages. Even in the '80s, Gil Scott Heron's lyrics said, "We've got to do something to save the children." Today, black music caters to and targets different age groups. It is the opposite now. Kids listen to adult versions of music and adults listen to clean versions of music.

Nowadays, our radio stations cater to what kids want to hear. There is something to be said for spiritual tips on a radio station at 6:30 a.m. to get your day started and "back that thang up" on that same station at 7 a.m. to get you pumped up for the day. I guess one way to look at it is that you need spiritual guidance when you rise because there is no telling what you are going to face throughout the remainder of your day.

My recommendation: Parents, put a foot down—your good foot, as James Brown used to say—and do not allow your kids to buy vulgar music. Sure, they will have opportunities to get their hands on it, anyway. The least we can do is let the kids know that we do not condone it. Who knows? The kids might respect a parent who takes a stance on the music issue.

Another recommendation: Very simply, take control of the stereos, particularly in the home and car. Turn the radio station to an oldies-but-goodies station. Need an excuse to give the kids? Let them know that this is what rappers listen to—'60s and '70s music to remake for them. Tell them that they can be on the cutting edge of old-school music, if there is such a thing.

Another recommendation: Turn your radios to talk radio sometimes. Kids nowadays think they know everything. Why not challenge them and their opinions on current issues that are discussed on talk radio.

Turn off the TV

Can we turn off the television? Studies show that black kids watch more than their share of television. Studies also show that black parents on average have the lowest expectations for their kids when it comes to grades in school. Lots of television watching plus low grade expectations equals a subpar student.

A few years back, the NAACP threatened to use boycotts, demonstrations, and lawsuits to protest the lack of minorities on television. Fighting for more minority roles in Hollywood is fine. But why not make the fight two-fold. The NAACP could initiate a "No-TV Week" and get kids to focus on school. They also could develop a program for adults to do something during "No-TV Week," such as reading to senior citizens. I think this would be nobler than fighting for Democrats.

My recommendation: Very simply, turn off the TV! At the very least, devise a television viewing schedule. Families can get the television guide on the weekend and decide what they are going to watch for the week.

Occasionally, leave the television off for a week or two, or even a month, save for the news. Watch the news in the morning and in the evening, and let that be it. During the time of no television, devise a schedule of other things to do. Going to the library would be one suggestion. How many families use their Blockbuster video cards more than their library cards? If a family is in this category, they need to turn the situation around immediately.

10

Random Topics

Here are a few random stories and thought-provoking topics.

*

While checking my daughter's school work one day, I came across a misspelled word. When I pointed it out, she said, "Daddy, that's okay because I don't have to turn that paper in to the teacher." I immediately responded by saying, "Taylor, every time you write you are taking a spelling test." Then I said, "Hey, that sounds pretty good. Write that down, Taylor." "Write what down?" she asked. "What I just said: 'Every time you write you are taking a spelling test.'"

We both started laughing about it, but that is something I preach to both of my children every time I see that one of them has misspelled a word.

*

The slavery reparations issue will never go away. The talk in the community for a while has been about every black person getting a check from Uncle Sam. That is how ordinary blacks envision reparations—every black person getting a check.

What do the so-called black leadership and other prominent blacks think about reparations? Randall Robinson, author of the book *The Debt*, and others have filed a lawsuit on behalf of black Americans seeking reparations. But in what form would the reparations be made? The black leadership and prominent groups such as the NAACP, the Rainbow Coalition, and others expect payments to be made to them, permitting them to spend the money where they see fit. So there is a big difference between what the average person, black or white, thinks will happen if reparations are paid.

*

When my kids were much younger, I read bedtime stories to them. They enjoyed listening to such great books as *The Berenstain Bears, Zack's Alligator*, and *McSpot's Hidden Spots*. Eventually I wrote a few short stories of my own, with my kids as the lead characters. They really enjoyed that. But once they got older and did not want to hear bedtime stories, what was I to do?

I came up with the bright idea of stepping up the reading material for bedtime stories. I began by reading current-events articles to them. While I read the newspaper during the day, if I came across an article that I felt would hold their attention, I would cut it out and save it for bedtime. The bedtime stories became a hit! I recommend this for anyone who has older kids.

Sometimes my kids would get so into it that they would

want to sit up and debate issues, which was great! But if I began to lose the debate, I could always say, "Okay kids, lights out! See you in the morning."

*

On October 15, 2003, Georgia Governor Sonny Perdue convened a Racial Reconciliation Forum at the Carter Library in Atlanta. Getting former President Jimmy Carter, a Democrat, involved was instrumental in bringing Democrats and Republicans together. The forum gave people who seem to care about race relations an opportunity to discuss racial issues that pertain to Georgia.

On the day of the event, state Representative Tyrone Brooks, a Democrat from Atlanta, made some comments that I found troubling and irresponsible. He was quoted in the *Atlanta Journal-Constitution* as saying, "I really believe people like President Carter, who has seen the transformation of the country over time, can talk to people who still hold racist views. Unfortunately, the people least likely to go are the ones who need it most."

Well, some people, both black and white, would say Brooks' comments apply to himself. After all, some people hold racist, bigoted, and prejudicial views regardless of their race. Besides, this was not a gathering of racists; this was a gathering of people we hoped wanted to better race relations. Maybe this was the reason Brooks decided not to attend. Fortunately, not all the members of the Georgia Association of Black Elected Officials, of which he is the president, heeded his way of thinking and stayed away from the forum.

After the introductions, welcome, and a review of the program, the forum got started with Dr. John Inscoe of the University of Georgia and Dr. Marcellus Barksdale of Morehouse College speaking about Georgia's slavery history. We all know slavery existed in Georgia, but it was good to hear these two learned individuals speak about slavery and enlighten us on some aspects of it and the Civil War. Dr. Inscoe stated that until the United States' defeat in Vietnam, Southerners were the only Americans who had lost a war. This makes some Southerners defensive about slavery and the Civil War.

Carter spoke about his upbringing in segregated rural Georgia. He had black friends and playmates, as well as black adults in his life who influenced him positively. Carter said there were basically five people who influenced him during his upbringing, and three of them were black individuals.

Perdue mentioned that his upbringing somewhat mirrored Carter's; he, too, had black friends growing up in segregated rural Georgia, even though they were born many years apart. I remember recently reading a biography of Perdue in the newspaper. It mentioned that his best friend, who was black, died when they were kids.

General Larry Ellis spoke about his tenure in the Army. He discussed Colin Powell's autobiography, in which Powell talked about being in the Army in Columbus, Georgia. Powell talked about the Army base being something of a safe haven, whereas the city of Columbus was a different story. Ellis stated that since Powell's days in Columbus, things have changed for the positive.

Robert Brown, president and chief executive officer of R L Brown & Associates, Inc., an architectural and construction management firm, spoke about the entrepreneurial spirit. He talked about his upbringing in Dublin, Georgia, and the black business owners in town. His mother was a seamstress and his father a contractor who often worked on the basis of a handshake and trust rather than a contract. He also spoke passionately about kids needing entrepreneurs as role models.

The audience question-and-answer segment was cordial and interesting. Four microphones were placed in the room and we lined up with our questions and comments. Unfortunately, time did not permit me to ask a question. With the session lasting only two hours, I think more time should have been allotted for the Q&A segment. Perhaps a smaller panel would have allowed more time for questions. Of course, every topic or question cannot be covered, regardless of the length of the forum.

Two people asked about an apology for slavery. I certainly do not need an apology from someone who did not have anything to do with slavery. Someone apologizing to me for something he or she had nothing to do with would seem to be appeasement, something I do not need. If anything, to say, "I am sorry for what your ancestors went through" would seem more appropriate. Then we could move on from there to rectify some of the lingering effects of slavery.

In regards to an apology, I remember how President Lincoln, in speeches and comments regarding the Civil War and slavery, stated that all the deaths and carnage the United States suffered was brought down on us because of slavery.

One lady asked about the number of black men in prison. Another person mentioned the number of blacks viewed negatively on the television news. When I got home that night, I turned on the TV to watch the 11 p.m. news report about the forum. First, however, there was a story about a black man who had turned himself in and admitted killing the 17-year-old mother of his 5-month-old baby twins. He had practically decapitated her. Could this news story answer the questions about black men in prison and negative views in the media? There is a misconception sometimes in the media about blacks, but stories like this do not help the situation.

One gentleman called for a Truth and Reconciliation hearing similar to what South Africa conducted under the leadership of Archbishop Desmond Tutu. Carter shot this down quickly, stating the difference between what happened in South Africa and here in the United States.

After the event, attendees were interviewed by news media representatives. One lady said Perdue spoke out of both sides of his mouth and one gentleman said Perdue was grandstanding. These were two examples of people who I feel did not come with open hearts. I believe they came with Democratic Party minds. They did not want to give Georgia's Republican governor a chance because they were of the opposite party.

Too many blacks hold the view that Republicans are racists. Sadly, some will never get past this. They refuse to look at the history of the two parties.

The day after the forum, I was quoted in the *Atlanta Journal-Constitution* as saying, "In two hours, you can't get everything done. I would have asked why black conservatives are not touted as role models in the black community... I'm constantly befuddled by people who demand an apology for slavery. People continually want an apology. Who should apologize?... We still need to move forward. Governor Perdue held his ground... As he said, 'This was the end of the beginning.'"

11

Writings: Speeches, Commentaries, and Opinions

———◆———

Here are some of my previous writings that I have penned over the years.

The following was written in response to the debate about what black people are to call ourselves.

African-American, Black, American: Which do you prefer?
(February 23, 1996)

Without trying to evade the question, I would like to say that it depends. I say this because I really don't think race and nationality should be juxtaposed. Why should they?

I recently grappled with this issue regarding what my wife and I teach our young children. Our foremost parental influence and persuasion is our race. We say to them, "My black

African prince or princess" or "What's up, black man?" Our kids even have been regulars at black art museums and galleries since their toddler days.

As the kids got older, we exposed them to being Americans. We've always had Old Glory displayed on our porch. We also have the Constitution and the Bill of Rights displayed in our home. Both my wife and I served our country in the military—Gail in the Army and I in the Air Force—so our kids have come to respect our troops. We even sent Valentine cards to our soldiers stationed in Bosnia. We're big Atlanta Braves fans, and through the baseball games, the children have learned to put their little right hands over their hearts and sing the national anthem.

One summer we went to the Atlanta International Culture Street Fest. There was a booth there that sold national flags. When Reggie and Taylor saw all the U.S. flags, they began shouting, "United States America flag, United States America flag!" I asked them to tell the booth owner how many stars and stripes are on the flag. The booth owner was so impressed with their enthusiasm for the flag that he gave each of them one of their own. This really made the kids' day. They marched around the festival and sang the national anthem as if they were the color guard at a Braves game.

Reflecting on these fond memories makes me realize that our kids are learning about their racial and familial heritage and, at the same time, are learning about patriotism and United States history without compromising one or the other.

In persuading and teaching our kids, I think that these two issues—race and nationality—should be taught separately because they are two of the many pillars that make up a person. These two pillars are strong and powerful enough to stand on their own merits. Rather than building kids' knowledge of these two issues on top of one another, we should teach them the difference between the two and build their knowledge on each issue.

By classifying ourselves as Black-American or African-American, Italian-American, etc., we are chipping away at these pillars and, in doing so, bringing each one down. For one thing, it tends to separate Americans into groups, making the different groups somewhat rivals or adversarial. When my family and I read about our troops in Bosnia, we are reading about American troops, not Greek-Americans or Irish-Americans. When we sent Valentine cards to our troops, we did not address them to African-Americans or German-Americans; they were addressed to "Our American Heroes."

I hope we can continue to keep teaching these two topics on separate planes. As for what I want my kids to call themselves, I'll try to leave that up to them.

The following article was written in response to numerous negative e-mails and comments circulated about the Debbie Allen and Steven Spielberg movie *Amistad*.

Amistad
(January 16, 1998)

Thank you, Debbie Allen and Steven Spielberg, for bringing the Amistad story to light. As a person who enjoys reading and informing himself on black history and the Constitution of the United States, I was taken aback that this story had never crossed my path.

I do not believe in my heart that Mr. Spielberg had any ulterior motive to equate Cinque to E.T. or to use him as a prop. It was the abolitionists and others during the time of slavery who used him as a necessary prop to prove and show how slavery was wrong.

Regarding when the Africans were talking among themselves and no translation was given, what translation was needed? Their dire circumstances were all I needed to come up with my own translation. People who have a problem about the lack of translation in these segments of the movie need to think that there must have been a point or meaning for this. Just use your own feelings and imagination to conjure up in your mind what they could have been saying.

There were no transcripts of the Africans' conversations for Mr. Spielberg to use—rather, he chose to put these segments in so the viewer perhaps could feel like he did or like I did when I was watching the movie: "What in the *! *@?#% did we do to deserve this *!*@?#% and what in the *!*@?#% are we going to do to get out from under these * ! *@?#% devils?" Come to think of it, if Mr. Spielberg had transcripts of some of their conversations, he might have had to bleep some words out, anyway. You can bet if I was one of the Africans, they would have had to change the rating of the movie from "R" to "X" because there would have been a whole lot of foul language going on.

And regarding not seeing the face of the white man who was whipping the Africans or seeing only the hands of a white man counting money: Let's face it, do you really need a face to see this hatred? What I picture in my mind in those scenes is not a character but a whole culture and society that condoned acts such as slavery itself, let alone the rapes and murders that took place. To this day, I am still puzzled about how our great forefathers could have written such beautiful documents as the Declaration of Independence and the Constitution of the United States and still have had slavery among them. Besides, a lot of the complainers call those non-faces "Whitey" anyway. What is the face of "Whitey"?

Again, I say thanks to Ms. Allen and Mr. Spielberg for bringing this story to light. Since it has come out, I have read about and have also seen a documentary on the Amistad, which was quite informative. It is not necessarily these two individuals' responsibility to teach us everything we need to learn about the Amistad, even though they took it upon themselves to help uncover this great story. It is up to us to make the movie just one of many forms of the way we educate ourselves about the Amistad.

The following was written in response to Internet search engines associating words such as *Kwanzaa* and *nigger*.

The N Word
(January 16, 1998)

I agree that the word *nigger* should not be used by search engines on the Internet. It is appalling to hear people use the word. What is even worse, though, are the harsh feelings that some people put behind the use of the word and the harsh reaction of the recipients, particularly if the recipients are black.

Some people (whites for example) spout the word to talk negatively about blacks, whereas other people use it in another way, such as the way some blacks use the word amongst themselves.

Regarding the words *nigger* and *Kwanzaa*, I do not understand how the two come up via a search engine (maybe in some twisted way they could come up in the Six Degrees of Separation game). However, I definitely understand the relationship of *nigger, rap*, and *hip-hop music*, because nigger is used not only in rap and hip-hop lyrics, but also in the culture of rap and hip-hop music listeners. (Have you seen the "Tommy RealNigger" t-shirts?) On the streets here in Atlanta, someone calling a friend "nigger" is equated with calling him "mister." It is often used as a way of giving someone respect, i.e., "What's up, my nigger!"

Regardless of how the word is used by our people, it should cease. Obviously, we cannot make anyone of any race or culture stop using it, but at least among back people it is merely a matter of educating ourselves to know that, on the whole, the word is demeaning to our race and should not be used. For whites and people of other races who use it when talking negatively about blacks, education is not the answer; it is a matter of them changing their hearts about how they feel about us. Such a change has to come from within them, with the help of some divine intervention.

Here again, though, is another instance in which we find ourselves criticizing, and rightfully so, the Yahoos and Web-crawlers of society, and then we have to turn around and criticize (or at least we *should* criticize) our own people for doing the exact same thing. At least some of us—Ward Connerly, Ken Hamblin, Thomas Sowell, et al— have the courage to criticize our own.

We are not going to get everyone to like and respect us, so about the best thing we can do for those who call us niggers is to pray for them.

The following is an e-mail that made the rounds during the time when President Clinton was in hot water over Monica Lewinsky.

Sent: Wednesday, February 03, 1999 8:21 a.m.
Subject: FW: Election Facts:
I just had to forward this. THIS IS DEEP!!!!! "Kind of Scary Huh?"
Subject: Election Facts:
This info is from an article in the *Western Legislatures* magazine. Thought you might find it interesting:

It is time to elect a world leader, and your vote counts. Here's the scoop on the three leading candidates. Decide whom you would choose:

Candidate A associates with ward heelers and consults with

astrologists. He's had two mistresses. He chain smokes and drinks 8 to 10 martinis a day.

Candidate B was kicked out of office twice, sleeps until noon, used opium in college and drinks a quart of brandy every evening.

Candidate C is a decorated war hero. He's a vegetarian, doesn't smoke, drinks an occasional beer and hasn't had any illicit affairs.

Which of these candidates is your choice??

Scroll down to find out!!

Candidate A Franklin D. Roosevelt

Candidate B Winston Churchill

Candidate C Adolf Hitler

After getting fed up with this nonsense, I decided to respond. I copied the following email to everyone who received the original email.

Date: Saturday, February 06, 1999 12:20 p.m.
Subject: Response to Election Facts E-mail
THIS IS DEEP!!!!! "Kind of Scary, huh?"
Yeah, right. The only thing that is deep and scary is that whoever wrote that (DEEP!!! and Scary) fell for it.

Quite frankly, I don't find any depth to these facts—if they are indeed facts. What I do find is a futile attempt to equate President Clinton's woes to those of others who were in high positions.

It is shameful to compare someone's faults and lawbreaking (lying under oath, witness tampering, obstruction of justice) with those of someone else we think highly of, like the way the liberals, particularly the White House, brought out Dr. Martin Luther King's trysts in order to equate President Clinton to Dr. King. People generally look at the good qualities of a person and try to attain those qualities and try not to duplicate the flaws. I think it is low to tarnish Dr. King in order to try to elevate President Clinton.

Now, regarding the three candidates, I could debunk all of this in one fell swoop by asking, "Did either of these candidates lie about their habits and/or peccadilloes under oath before one of the three branches of government (judicial) that was set up by the Constitution?" Actually, I need two fell swoops. The other one is, being that Candidates B and C did not hold office in the United States, whatever they did is moot because the laws and expectations for an American president did not apply to them.

But let's look at your three candidates anyway for some clarifications of history.

Candidate A (Franklin D. Roosevelt) associates with ward heelers and consults with astrologists. He's had two mistresses. He chain smokes and drinks 8 to 10 martinis a day.

Was Roosevelt ever summoned before a court of law and questioned about ward heelers (whatever those are). Was he questioned before a court regarding astrologists, mistresses, smoking, drinking, blah blah blah. I think not. Bam! I just blew that one out the sky. But wait, I have two more nonsense utterances to shoot down. Hold on.

Candidate B (Winston Churchill) was kicked out of office twice, sleeps until noon, used opium in college and drinks a quart of brandy every evening.

Let's try a little Clinton butchering of the English language. Was that noon Washington, D.C., time or noon London time when he woke up. It depends on which noon you are talking about (it depends on what the meaning of *is* is). Also, you did not clarify whether he inhaled the opium or not. And which is more, a quart or a liter? You see how silly this can get when trying to compare Clinton's screw-ups to others' screw-ups? POW! Another one bites the dust! Two down, one to go. (This is so easy.)

Candidate C (Adolf Hitler) is a decorated war hero. He's a vegetarian, doesn't smoke, drinks an occasional beer and hasn't had any illicit affairs.

Hitler served in the military. Clinton didn't serve. But to his credit, he did get served by Monica Lewinsky, et al. According to the federal laws on sexual harassment in the government workplace, it was illegal to have sex with interns and/or your subordinates. Oh, and Clinton wasn't a decorated war hero, but he did say he decorated his El Camino car with Astroturf in the back for the girls.

Hitler was a vegetarian. So what? Clinton eats at McDonald's.

One other important fact of the comparison of Hitler to Clinton. In both cases, the people just stood idly by while their two leaders did their destruction. And I am sure that Clinton really appreciates being compared to Hitler.

Boom! Three for three!

So when you say, "Kind of Scary, huh?" I say, yes, it is scary that an adult can fall for this trickery when my 6-year-old and 8-year-old children know that their beloved president is in trouble because he lied. It's scary also that so many American citizens, let alone foreigners, succumb to the brainwashing of a political party that will do anything to keep their party leader from being defeated rather than doing what is right by our U.S. Constitution.

R. Bohannon

Questions? Comments? E-mail me at rbohannon@earthlink. net.

I did not receive any e-mails about this, though I did receive a call from the lady who forwarded the original e-mail to me. She scolded me and told me to never send out an e-mail like that to her friends. Funny, I have not heard from her since.

The following is my response to an e-mail titled "Getting

Paid in the Black Community" that circulated amongst blacks in January 2000:

It's Not All About Getting Paid
(January 9, 2000)
Without being disrespectful, I would like to discuss some elements of your "Getting Paid in the Black Community" e-mail.

First and foremost, give us a little credit. Black people who earn millions of dollars a year are not the only blacks who are getting paid. You do not have to be a millionaire to be successful. Second, it is not just sports personalities, entertainers, and criminals who are getting paid as you stated.

Let's look at sports. Here in the United States, black athletes are basically getting paid in three main sports: basketball, football, and baseball. I do not feel the need to do any research to find out the total number of black athletes in these sports. But in comparison to the number of black people here in the United States, that number is miniscule, a mere drop in the bucket. Yet I see and know of a lot of successful black people who are not in sports. (Come check out the ATL!)

In saying this, my point is that there are blacks all across the United States who are getting paid even though they are not in sports, entertainment, or the criminal world. And save for the criminal profession, these professions are not all that bad. Besides, white people are not the only ones who like being entertained. You stated, "Historically the white community has enlisted the black community to entertain white people." Well, my friends and I are certainly going to watch the Super Bowl while kicking back and jamming to maybe George Clinton, Bootsy, or Stevie Wonder.

In response to your statement about corrupt politicians, the only thing I can say is that I am not sure whether you are upset that white politicians are better at being corrupt than our black politicians. Go figure. Besides, I think that a corrupt black politician harms our community more than a white politician.

You posed the question, "Why don't black scientists, teachers, and business owners get paid?" Well, some of them do—and some have longer careers than most athletes and entertainers. You also say, "The white community and any other minority community in comparison to blacks would not project sports, entertainment, and crime as their top three wage earners." Well, I am here to say that the black community does not do that—you do.

Wait a minute! You know, it just dawned on me that you are saying that criminals rank in the top three in wage earnings amongst black people. You have got to be kidding! Where do you live? Do you reside in the United States? Certainly not the ATL! Come on! You have got to be joking. Now I don't know whether to reply to your article or not because it seems like one of those Internet jokes that get passed around. I guess I will respond anyway, just in case someone did not get the joke. You are very funny!

Regarding athletes and entertainers, some of them have been very instrumental in the progress of blacks as a whole. There have been quite a few athletes and entertainers who not only have had little black kids dreaming of playing sports or dancing and singing, they have had kids and adults dreaming and aspiring to do well in all kinds of endeavors. Muhammad Ali did not inspire all black kids, especially black girls, to become boxers. Well, I take that back a little since his and Joe Frazier's daughters became boxers. People like Althea Gibson, Marian Anderson, and Wendell Scott got us to think about ourselves and what we could become or achieve within our own worlds, not just theirs. Curtis Mayfield, God rest his soul, got us thinking about who we are as a people, the proud people that we are. Thanks, Mr. Mayfield.

I know there is still work to be done in our community,

but let's not take such a broad, dim view of our community. That is, if you can find our so-called "black community." We have disseminated virtually everywhere in these great United States. Black people are successful in practically every profession that is known to man. We may not have as many successful people as whites do, but we are making progress. So in our struggle to reach higher ground, let's not condemn our black community and the people who are trying to be successful, monetarily or otherwise.

And that crack about the criminals in the top three wage earners still has me laughing! It was a joke. Wasn't it?

The following is my response to people who tend to put sports on a low echelon when something tragic happens here in America.

The Importance of Sports in a World of Terror
(December 1, 2001)
The pre-game and post-game ceremonies, as well as the Army-Navy game itself, put sports in a different perspective for me. The seniors in the game were playing in the last game of their football careers. They will soon be off on a new career.

The game meant the world to the players, as well as to their classmates, families, and fans. To see all the 18- to 20-year-old kids in the stands having a great time, knowing that they could be off to fight for their country one day in the near future—I must say, it was touching.

Regardless of which team won or lost, the game was probably a morale booster for U.S. servicemen and women everywhere. It definitely was uplifting for this Air Force veteran. Knowing that bright young people like those players and fans have chosen to serve our country lets me know that there are a lot of people, young and old, who love their country and the freedom we enjoy here.

We have the freedom to strive to be television stars or couch potatoes. We have the freedom to strive to be professional athletes or sports fans.

Every time something catastrophic happens here in America, we are reminded by some in the media how little sports means in the overall scheme of things. I beg to differ. It's not a matter of whether we could live without sports and other entertainment. It is a matter of whether we would want to live in a place where we were not permitted to be an athlete, sports fan, or couch potato.

On the news on November 30, it was reported that the Marines were basically on hold and bored in Afghanistan. So what did they do to try to beat boredom? They start getting sports scores reported from back home; football, basketball, hockey, etc. They wanted to keep up with the so-called frivolous things from back home. But who knows? Keeping up with the scores might have let them know everything was somewhat all right on the home front. Imagine what kind of bummer it would have been for our troops abroad if the World Series had been canceled because America had not recovered from September 11. That wouldn't necessarily have been the news they would have wanted to hear from home.

Sports and entertainment can represent many different things to different people. It could be a sense of freedom— freedom to be able to pursue happiness. It could also be a big morale booster for the military and civilians. So I say, yes, sports means a lot to this country. Just ask the fans of the Army and Navy ... game, that is.

The following are my comments on "The State of Black America Forum" that Tavis Smiley hosted.

The State of Black America Forum
(February 3, 2003)

Mr. Smiley, I applaud your efforts to organize "The State of Black America Forum" that was on C-SPAN on Saturday, February 3, 2003.

However, I think the panel bought into the notion that we should blame our problems on others (Republicans) rather than coming to solutions that can help us regardless of Republicans. During the forum, it took until 11:14 a.m. for someone (T.D. Jakes) to point out that with either Republican or Democratic administrations, our problems still exist—the same problems we blacks faced thirty or forty years ago. Even Sonia Sanchez later said that the same things were discussed twenty years ago.

Some of the issues I would like to discuss are listed below:

Crime and drugs: Rather than keep pointing out the fact that more blacks than whites are put in jail for crimes in proportion to our populations, why not put the focus on black individuals and our communities doing what they can to minimize the crimes, particularly black-on-black crimes. Rather than keep arguing the point and focusing on cocaine users (mainly looked at as being white people) and crack users (mainly looked at as being black people), we should focus on encouraging blacks not to get involved with cocaine or crack. I feel that doing this would make the argument about cocaine and crack sentencing moot. The way the argument is being played out now, it is as if we blacks want a level playing field on sentencing so that we can continue to use crack. We may get incarcerated for breaking the drug laws, but as long as we are sentenced the same as whites, we won!

Crack is harmful not only to our bodies but to our black communities. Why not leave crack to the whites or whomever? If not one black person in America used crack, that would be a victory for black individuals and our black communities.

I know that it is a large task, but by and large, we left glue sniffing and toad licking to the whites.

Ghettos and other poor neighborhoods: It is a great thing to have programs to help families that live in ghettos and poor neighborhoods. On the other hand, there should be something in place that actually gets people moved out of poor neighborhoods, thereby reducing public housing.

It seems sometimes that the issue has gotten turned around. Some people take it as a success that lots of new prisons are being built nationwide. The same goes for the increasing number of services we as a nation provide to citizens. The idea seems to be that the more services that are provided, the more success. However, the less the nation has to provide, the more successful we all will become.

I also would like to bring up the fact that there are conservative blacks in this country. However, out of all the people on the stage, including Tom Joyner, Raymond Brown, and yourself, Ken Blackwell was the only conservative during the first session. It also must be noted that the highest ranking black elected official in the country was on during the second session, and he is a Republican.

I would like to see a forum with the likes of Dr. Thomas Sowell, Dr. Walter Williams, Joseph Perkins, Larry Elder, Peter Kirsanow, Ken Hamblin, and others. These black men are indeed black people, and they have different views regarding our race—different than those of the panelists of the forum, save for Ken Blackwell. After all, as T.D. Jakes stated, "We all don't think alike."

Mr. Smiley, I must admit that I haven't tracked your rise in the media, but it seems to me, and I apologize if I am wrong, that the higher you have gone, the more you have espoused the Democratic Party mantra, at least on your BET show. The same goes for Tom Joyner. Mr. Smiley, I saw you speak in Charlotte, North Carolina, at the For Sisters Only Trade Show

(Roger Troutman's last performance), and you surprised me when you spoke out negatively about Bill Clinton. Then I thought, "Why speak out negatively about Bill Clinton in front of a limited audience but not on your show?" That is more evidence for me and others that you are more loyal to a party than to black people. It also lends more truth to the notion that the Democratic Party gets people like Jesse Jackson, Al Sharpton, and other liberal blacks, including you, to lead the black masses to the Democratic Party for the benefit of the party and not for the benefit of the blacks.

I think that it is fantastic that blacks are getting involved politically. But I also feel that a number of blacks are getting into politics to see what they can get out of government and how government can correct wrongs that we as blacks have had a great hand in.

I know that people can get into politics for whatever reason, but there is another party out there. When black liberals paint the Republican Party as racist, the black masses tend to believe it. I personally do not believe that the Republican Party as a whole is racist. We blacks need to come to the realization that regardless of how we feel about the Republican Party, it is a legitimate party in America. Moreover, if we feel that it is racist, why not join it in order to eradicate the racism that we feel exists in that party. After all, there is no fee to join the party. You already know the old saying about putting all our eggs in one basket.

As long as we blame the white man, particularly the white Republican man, forums such as the "The State of Black America Forum" will be time ill spent on C-SPAN.

The following is a song titled "Shock and Awe" that I wrote in April 2003 during the height of the Iraq War:

Fool you want to mess with me

You better check my history.
Just like in Baghdad
if you make me real mad
I'll make your whole crew sad.

Brother I'm a soldier
I thought Master P told ya.

Step to me
I'll treat you like an Iraqi combatant
I'll leave your ass flattened.

Just like the military
if I find it necessary
I'll say forget the law and
bring on the shock and awe.

If you mess with me
I'll make you bleed.
I'll shock and awe ya.
I'll shock and awe ya.

If you step to my crew
We'll split you in two.
We'll shock and awe ya.
We'll shock and awe ya.

So what's it gonna be
MIA, KIA or should I just make you a POW?
Then no one can save you but George W.

Don't try to hide in the day
and then
when it gets night

you want to fight.
I'm outta sight
I got too much might
Because I'm right.

Just like the Army in Basra
I got the night-vision goggles
Yeah, I can still see ya.
I'm not here to playa hate ya.
But like the Marines, I'm here to liberate ya.
But if you mess with me
Like Bush on Saddam
I'll drop that bomb.
You know the one I'm talking about
the MOAB, The Mother of All Bombs

If you mess with me
I'll make you bleed.
I'll shock and awe ya.
I'll shock and awe ya.

If you step to my crew
We'll split you in two.
We'll shock and awe ya.
We'll shock and awe ya.

To me you're like a CNN embed.
You're coming to me with
that "He said, she said."
Just like my boys in the Air Force
I'll make your whole crew very porous.

I'm coming crazy with a daisy cutter.
It's cuttin' through you like

a knife through butter.
Then I'm dippin' in the Southern
No-Fly Zone and I'm gone.

Now after all that
If you still want to combat
Like the U.S. Navy
I'll bring it like Jay-z
with a Tomahawk cruise missile.
For shizzle my nizzle

Yeah, yeah, don't try to hide. We see you up there in Kirkuk,
Mosul, Tikrit. I bet you thought we couldn't even pronounce
your cities. But we've been studying you for over twelve years.
Got the GPS right on your behind.

Coalition forces, thanks for holding it down. USA, Australia,
the UK, Spain. Central Command—General Franks. General
Brooks—you're doin' it, brother. The Pentagon. Rumsfeld—
give 'em hell. Shouts out to my old crew, the 89th MAW Air
Force One Presidential Wing at Andrews Air Force Base.

Shouts out to all the troops in Bahrain, Kuwait, Qatar, United
Arab Emirates, Oman. You're doin' it. Can't forget Diego Gar-
cia out there in the Indian Ocean, slangin' those Tomahawks.

This is for you, you're holding it down.
Chief Warrant Officer Ronald Young. Shoshana Johnson and
all the rest. Welcome home.

We'll see you back in the states.
Peace—in the Middle East.

The following is a response to Clarence Page, a syndicated columnist who wrote about role models or the lack thereof.

Hear hip hop's not-so-hidden message
(September 15, 2003)
I've got three role models for today's generation who, as you put it, "can help them lift their eyes out of the gutter and aim them toward the stars": Dr. Condoleezza Rice, Justice Clarence Thomas, and Secretary of State Colin Powell. The problem is that your generation is not fond of conservative blacks.

There is something ironic, though, when you look at the political aspect of this issue. The same rappers who put out negative music are used to recruit voters for the Democratic Party, the same party that does not want our black youth looking up to the likes of Rice, Thomas, and Powell. When we as blacks rise above political parties, our eyes will be open to myriad role models, conservative blacks included.

The following are Toastmasters speeches I have done:

The Greatest Legal Document Ever Written
(October 30, 2002)
Prior to my speech, I handed out bookmarkers with the preamble printed on them.
That would be the Constitution of the United States. I chose to speak about the Constitution because I consider myself a Constitution enthusiast. The Constitution is not perfect; it has its flaws. This is because man is not perfect, and the Constitution was written by man. But it is a document on which many countries around the world have modeled their own constitutions. They realize the need for a constitution that puts the people first, as opposed to putting their dictators or even their religions first—countries such as Cuba, Iraq, and Saudi Arabia. When constitutional issues are decided, some I agree with

and some I do not. But at least the Constitution exists to give some guidance so we may live in harmony to the best of our abilities.

"We the People of the United States, in Order to form a more perfect Union, establish Justice, ensure domestic Tranquility, provide for the common defence, promote the general Welfare, and secure the Blessings of Liberty to ourselves and our Posterity, do ordain and establish this Constitution for the United States of America."

Just a side note—as you can see on the bookmarker, during the time the Constitution was written, defence was spelled with a "C."

The Constitution consists of the preamble, seven articles, the signatures, and twenty-seven amendments. Save for the amendments, it has 4,440 words. There's not much to it when you look at it.

On May 25, 1787, in Independence Hall, the Constitutional Convention opened with a quorum of seven states. Eventually, twelve of the thirteen states were represented by men of valor. Rhode Island did not send delegates. The state's leaders did not want to be part of a conspiracy to overthrow their nascent government.

The delegates met in secrecy. Sentries were posted at the entrance to keep out the citizens and the press. The delegates felt that if they met in secrecy, they could express their feelings and concerns without being swayed by outside influences.

George Washington was elected president of the convention. He sat in a nice wooden chair. The chair had a carving of the sun on the back of it. In the summer of 2000, I, along with my kids and some friends, visited Philadelphia. We went to Independence Hall. For me, one of the highlights of the trip was seeing the chair that George Washington used and seeing that sun carved in the chair.

The delegates debated several issues. One issue was how

the states would be represented. The most populated states said that the more people they had, the more representatives they should have in Congress. The smaller states did not agree. Eventually, the delegates decided to have a bicameral system consisting of a Senate and a House of Representatives. The more populated the state, the more congressmen the state would have to represent its citizens. The Senate would consist of two senators per state.

Another issue was the question of what should be done about slavery. Now that was a tough one. In the Constitution, blacks were counted as three-fifths of a person. I have heard scores of people say that it is a shame that the Constitution didn't recognize blacks as a whole person. But after research, I somewhat disagree.

First of all, if this issue had not been resolved to satisfy the Southern delegates, they more than likely would have walked away from the bargaining table and left without the Constitution we have today. Thus, the Southern states could have continued the slavery institution without any opposition. So there is no telling how long slavery would have existed without a new Constitution.

The delegates had already decided that the more people a state had, the more representatives it would have in Congress. The South recognized slaves as property but, at the same time, the Southern delegates wanted the slaves to be counted as part of their population. The Northern delegates realized that if the slaves were counted as part of the population, the South would get more Congressmen who would continue to vote to keep slavery and perhaps never would abolish it. So it was the Northern delegates, who were against slavery, who came up with what is called the three-fifths compromise. Along with the three-fifths compromise, the delegates decided that the importation of slaves would end in 1808.

After months of haggling over a cornucopia of issues and

showing great tenacity, the delegates finally completed the Constitution. Thirty-nine of the forty-two delegates lined up in geographical order, from New Hampshire to Georgia, and signed the Constitution. When Benjamin Franklin got to the table, he looked up with tears in his scintillating eyes and said, "During all this time, I've been looking at that sun on George Washington's chair and didn't know if it was rising or setting. But today, I can say it is a rising sun."

Since the Bill of Rights, more amendments have been added. Some amendments specifically pertain to us. The 13th Amendment abolished slavery. The 14th Amendment struck down the three-fifths compromise and granted people equal protection under the law. During World War I, Congress decided to add the 16th Amendment, which gave Congress the power to collect income taxes to help fund the war. As we know, we won the war, but the government is still collecting income taxes. The 18th Amendment prohibited the sale and distribution of intoxicating liquors. But fortunately for quite a few of us here, the 21st Amendment repealed the 18th Amendment. The 19th Amendment allowed women to vote.

So take time out to read the Constitution. It can be read in about thirty minutes. It is the oldest and shortest written Constitution of any government in the world. Then, when you go to vote next Tuesday, you will have a great barometer, the greatest legal document ever written, the Constitution of the United States. May God bless America.

Toastmasters—Star-Spangled Banner
(February 2, 2003)
Good afternoon, everyone. Thanks for coming. This is my third speech. The previous speeches dealt with patriotism, Americana, and the greatest legal document ever written, the Constitution.

For this speech, I initially wanted to go in a different direction. I say "in a different direction" because it was going to be about baseball game outings with my kids, and the joy and togetherness those outings bring. You can hardly get more Americana than baseball. But with the tragic accident of the *Columbia* space shuttle this past Saturday, I felt drawn back to the patriotism and Americana theme.

As I viewed the editorial cartoon by Mike Luckovich in Sunday's newspaper, I began to think about what it meant to me. I also thought about what I could extrapolate out of the tragedy that would be uplifting and inspirational, something I could convey and share with my kids and others.

At first glance, you see seven stars representing the seven astronauts streaming from outer space that are about to spangle a blank blue field of the United States flag that is flying at half-staff. The stars represent Commander Rick Husband, Michael Anderson, David Brown, Kalpana Chawla, Laurel Clark, William McCool, and Ilan Ramon. There is even a Star of David representing Ramon, who was an Israeli.

The fifty stars on our United States flag represent the fifty states. The states in turn represent their citizenry. The flag's blue field symbolizes heaven. Each and every day, the blue field of Old Glory starts as a blank starless canvas. America wakes up each morning, and as the day goes by, people taking on small and big endeavors—the things that make America and its ideas work—spangle the blank blue field. On February 1, the *Columbia* space shuttle crew spangled Old Glory.

The stars represent not only the extraordinary citizens and the things they do, but also the ordinary people and the tasks we do to make America what it is—people like us, who get up each day and exercise our God-given freedom and rights to go about our lives productively.

As evidenced by the loss of the *Columbia* space shuttle crew, Old Glory is spangled each day by people of all races, of both sexes, and of all sorts of nationalities. To me, this is evidence that this is not just a country that belongs to Americans, but also a country that belongs to God.

My daughter, Taylor, who is 10 years old, has said since she was about 5-years-old that she would like to become an astronaut. I would say, "Yeah, Taylor, that would be cool if you could become an astronaut." But as parents know, kids change career dreams a thousand times. But whenever there would be an inkling of seriousness coming from her about a particular career, I would always tell her how to become that hair stylist, comedian, or astronaut that she wanted to become: Do well in school and get not just good grades but great grades, and then move on and excel in college.

Her interest in an astronaut career has waned somewhat. A couple of years ago, her cousin told her that she could die in space as an astronaut. I would try to contend with this by explaining to her that you can die working in any career field.

Taylor's fourth-grade class watched the *Columbia* space shuttle launching on January 16, so I knew that when I talked to her again, the space shuttle disaster would be our first topic of conversation. Fortunately, I had time to come up with a decent parental response. I told her that if you have a dream that you would like to fulfill, you should pursue it. When the *Challenger* space shuttle disaster occurred in 1986, not only were some of the future astronauts of the *Columbia* emboldened and filled with a desire to go into space, but numerous other people showed persistence and chose to stick with their dream of working with the space program to try to make it better. They tried to make it better by striving for excellence and perfection to make their job and the space program in general safer. As with the *Challenger* and now the *Columbia* disaster, there will be kids worldwide who will be heartened and even more focused on following their dreams of space exploration.

So I say to you all, take time out of your busy lives once in a while to think about your own star on the flag, your place in this world, and how well illuminated your star will be today on Old Glory—on this earth.

May God bless America.

12

Where Do I Go from Here?

———◆———

I first must say that from here I hope to get closer to God to prepare and shield myself from the arrows that no doubt will be fired my way on account of this book. Hopefully, my debates and arguments with Mom have steeled me to withstand my opponents.

I will continue to educate and inform my children and myself on American history, the Constitution, and politics, as well as debate others about my conservative viewpoint. I will remain conservative because of my core beliefs, regardless of politics.

I am sure this book will be controversial to some, particularly black Democrats. It will surely spark debates in several households across our fruited plains. Much of the book is debatable, which I welcome; I am prepared to debate and hash out ideas and issues. However, I must admit, the name calling—"Uncle Tom," "sell-out," etc.—and put-downs from my own brothers and sisters, particularly from the likes of Julian Bond and Kweisi Mfume, will take some getting used to. I can only pray about it. I hearken back to Mfume's comments about black Republican organizations being puppets of white Republican organizations. Isn't that the pot calling the kettle black? Wasn't the National Association for the Advancement of Colored People founded by whites? Even today, Democratic supporters and groups such as white billionaire George Soros and MoveOn.org, whose sole reason for existence is to see President Bush ousted, fund the NAACP.

Over the past few years, a number of people have asked me if I will ever run for office. No, because I cannot see myself on a campaign trail asking for campaign dollars. I do see myself continuing to educate others, particularly kids, on American history and the Constitution. Most importantly, I want to continue to exercise my constitutional right under the 15th Amendment, which states, "The right of citizens of the United States to vote shall not be denied or abridged by the United States or by any State on account of race, color or previous condition of servitude."

I just thought I would take one last opportunity to drop some constitutional knowledge on you.

Appendix

Recommended Reading
and Web Sites

—◦—

The following are some authors and their books that I recommend reading:

James A. Baker, III, *The Politics of Diplomacy*
H.W. Brands, *The First American*
Ann Coulter, *Treason*
Nick Del Calzo and Peter Collier, *Medal of Honor*
Burke Davis, *Black Heroes of the American Revolution*
Larry Elder, *The Ten Things You Can't Say in America*
Paul Finkelman, *Slavery and the Founders*
Ken Hamlin, *Pick a Better Country*
Sean Hannity, *Deliver Us from Evil*

Phil Kent, *The Dark Side of Liberalism*
Mark R. Levin, *Men in Black*
Rush Limbaugh, *See, I Told You So* and *The Way Things Ought To Be*
David McCullough, *John Adams* and *1776*
John McWhorter, *Authentically Black*
Zell Miller, *A National Party No More* and *Corp Values*
Bill O'Reilly, *Who's Looking Out for You?*
Thomas Paine, *Common Sense*
Star Parker, *Pimps, Whores and Welfare Brats*
Reverend Jesse Lee Peterson, *Scam*
Alexis de Tocqueville, *Democracy in America*
George Washington, *Farewell Address*
J.C. Watts, Jr., *What Color Is a Conservative?*
Martha Zoller, *Indivisible*

Historical Documents:
The Magna Carta
The Declaration of Independence
The Articles of Confederation
The Federalist Papers
The Constitution
Red Skelton's Rendition of the Pledge of Allegiance

Below is a list of conservative columnists who can be found on the Internet:
Mike S. Adams
Neal Boortz
Ward Connerly
Ann Coulter
Larry Elder
Ken Hamlin
David Limbaugh
Rich Lowry

Michelle Malkin
Star Parker
Joseph Perkins
Dennis Prager
Thomas Sowell
Armstrong Williams
Walter E. Williams

Below are Web sites that are quite informative because they
have links to columnists and other Web sites:
boortz.com
drudgereport.com
jewishworldreview.com
newsmax.com
rushlimbaugh.com
townhall.com

Listed below are television programs on Fox News that are out
of the mainstream media. Fox is considered conservative, par-
ticularly because conservatives are represented on Fox more
so than on other television networks.
Fox & Friends
Special Report with Brit Hume
The O'Reilly Factor
Hannity & Colmes
Fox News Sunday with Chris Wallace
The Beltway Boys

Below are radio talk-show hosts who are quite informative.
They have great debates and they delve out great information
on current events.
Bill Bennett
Neal Boortz
Ken Hamlin

Sean Hannity
Laura Ingraham
Rush Limbaugh
Kim Peterson
Michael Savage
Martha Zoller

I am sure I have left out a number of books, Web sites, bloggers, radio hosts, and other media outlets. But the lists above will give you a great start. The people and sources above all can eventually lead to other sources that will provide a wealth of information.

About the Author

R eginald Bohannon, 45, was born and raised in Lexington, North Carolina, home of furniture making and
great barbecue.

Reginald served seven years in the United States Air Force,
including three at Little Rock Air Force Base in Arkansas. He
quickly rose through the ranks and earned a "Special Duty
Assignment" to the Air Force One Presidential Wing under
President Ronald Reagan at Andrews Air Force Base in Maryland.

Reginald currently resides in Atlanta, Georgia. He is the
father of a son, Reginald, Jr., and a daughter, Taylor.

ISBN 141207939-X